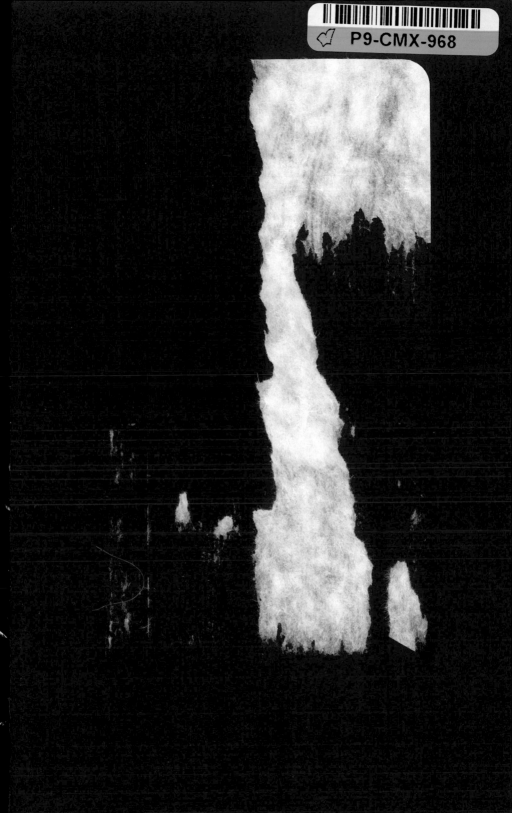

Eurocommunism
and the State

Eurocommunism
and the State

Santiago Carrillo

Westport, Connecticut

This material was first published in Spanish by
Editorial Critica, Barcelona, as *Eurocommunismo y Estado.*

The translation from the Spanish by Nan Green and A. M. Elliott
is used with permission of Lawrence and Wishart Ltd, London.

Library of Congress Catalog Card Number: 78-51455
ISBN: 0-88208-093-8 (cloth edition)   0-88208-094-6 (paperback edition)

1 2 3 4 5 6 7 8 9 10

LAWRENCE HILL&CO.

24 Burr Farms Road, Westport, Connecticut 06880

Distributed by Whirlwind Book Co., 80 Fifth Ave., New York, N. Y. 10011

Jacket design by Robert McLeod.
Jacket photograph courtesy United Press International.
Manufactured in the United States by R. R. Donnelley & Sons.

Eurocommunism
and the State

This book is dedicated to T. and R.; to B.;
and to Carmen, Santiago, Pepe and Jorge who
helped me so much

Contents

Eurocommunism and the State

'perturbed' if his explanation did not seem sufficiently clear and convincing, 'because the question of the State is a most difficult and complex one, perhaps one that more than any other has been confused by bourgeois scholars, writers and philosophers' (Lenin, *Collected Works*, vol. 29, p. 470).

To this I would humbly add, on the basis of my own inadequate self-education, that the Marxist texts themselves are fraught with obscurities and even sometimes contradictions – at least formal ones – which can arouse doubts in the reader or at any rate give him food for thought. The subject is so complicated! And if from theory we pass to practice, the contradictions and confusions increase, since between the transitional socialist State described by Lenin in his classical work on the subject and the State which subsequently came into being even in his own lifetime – not to mention after his death! – there are fundamental differences.

The reader may perhaps be surprised at the frequency with which in the following pages I use the term 'Eurocommunism'. It is very fashionable, and though it was not coined by the Communists and its scientific value may be doubtful, it has acquired a meaning among the public and, in general terms, serves to designate one of the current communist trends. If it is still rather imprecise, a part of this imprecision corresponds to what is still undecided, exploratory, in this trend which has up till now manifested itself more as a serious, self-critical rectification of policy than in theoretical elaboration. This demonstrates once again that practice is usually ahead of theory, that theory is a generalisation of practice, though practice gains solidity and basic content when theory confirms it, gives it scientific precision and extends and clarifies its influence.

However, the policy and theoretical implications which justify 'Eurocommunism' describe a tendency in the modern progressive and revolutionary movement that is endeavouring to get to grips with the realities of our continent – though in essence it is valid for all developed capitalist countries – and adapt to them the development of the world revolutionary process characteristic of our time.

The real problems and contradictions, public and notorious, that exist in the world communist and workers' movement, are a reflection of that process. Contradictions of State are apparent

Introduction

Early in 1976 an exceptional set of circumstances provided me with the free time and a suitable frame of mind for tackling one of the most confused and difficult questions confronting a communist today.

When I crossed the frontier into Spain in February, I knew that for a shorter or longer period my presence would not be tolerated by the authorities, and that I should be obliged to live strictly underground. Though my intention was gradually to overcome this situation and reassert my rights as a Spanish citizen, while taking an active part in the political work involved in preparing a Communist Party suited to conditions of democracy, it was certain that I would have to do this in a way which would leave me some time to go more deeply into ideas which had been worrying me for some time, and to write about them.

A generous friend placed his varied and well-stocked library at my disposal; in it there were many books dealing with the State – the subject which was preoccupying me – though because of the restrictions of the Spanish censorship not all were of the Marxist character I would have needed in order to provide exact quotations and sources, and to check my memory. Among this reading matter, some was of little use to me and some very valuable. Had I been free, I might perhaps have been able to use more substantial sources which would have been still more helpful; but then it would have been difficult to find the time in which to do it. So I had to take the rough with the smooth.

On 11 July 1919, in a lecture he gave at Sverdlov University, entitled 'The State', Lenin warned his audience not to be in them, some originating in the particular ways in which the formation of those states was carried out under the previous social forms, in which forced annexations played no small part, creating political realities which do not always correspond to ethnic and historical ones. There also enter into them, superimposed on them, new contradictions arising from differing interests as regard a variety of problems, and from the fact, to which Lenin referred, that the proletariat *does not become a band of saints* through the simple fact of having taken power. Moreover, the problems and contradictions of the working-class and communist movement arise from the variety of roads and concrete conditions, and the weight of cultural traditions and economic and social structures, which engender real political and ideological tendencies that acquire great influence when the revolutionary process embraces the whole world in all its enormous diversity.

These tendencies are a reality today, and will not be resolved by 'decrees of unification' or by excommunications; they will gradually be *extinguished* in the long process of the universalisation of society, of culture, of the socialist economic and political system – a process the duration of which nobody can predict.

So 'Eurocommunism' forces itself upon us as a reality, as long as we cannot find a better definition. It is as well to give a warning, however, that this tendency is not an organisation, nor does it even have a common programme, though it does undeniably possess a specific nature which shows itself in different ways at international conferences, such as that of the European Communist Parties in June 1976 in East Berlin.

It is not a matter of a *third road*, to use a term favoured by popular journalism. For if we were to set out to enumerate the different roads being followed in the world revolutionary process, there would be many more than three. Nor is it a question of a retreat to social-democratic positions, or of a denial of the historical reasons which justified the birth of communist parties.

It must be recognised, however, that the approach to the problem of the State in the following pages involves a difference from Lenin's theses of 1917 and 1918. These were applicable to Russia and theoretically to the rest of the world at that time.

They are not applicable today because they have been overtaken in the circumstances of the developed capitalist countries of western Europe. What has made them inapplicable is the change in economic structures and the objective expansion of the progressive social forces, the development of the productive forces (including nuclear energy), the advance of socialism and decolonisation, and the defeat of fascism in the Second World War.

It may strike some people as blasphemous to read that some of Lenin's theses are out of date; there are those who are unaware that Lenin said the same thing about Marx, and that the Soviet successors of Lenin openly revised some of his theses.

My work on this subject was interrupted when I was arrested in Madrid on 22 December 1976. A week later, now that I am leaving prison to become a legal citizen, I no longer have the time, for the present, to continue polishing it. I confine myself to making a rapid revision for the press, confident that the book's gaps and shortcomings will be overcome in the course of the debate which will arise round a subject which is of such decisive importance.

December 1976

1

The State versus Society

From the very outset, I want to lose no time in announcing the
vexed question which I intend simply to pose, seeking to
initiate a debate in which clearer and better-equipped minds
will continue the work, even if it means the demolition of my
own efforts. It is the question of the State, democracy and
socialism, in the specific perspective posed by the Communist
Party of Spain and, by and large, in similar terms by other
communist parties like the Italian, Japanese, French, British,
Swedish, etc., which, without trying to set an *example*, are now
tracing a line of renewal in the international working-class and
communist movements, in the context of the economic, social
and political characteristics of the economically-developed
capitalist countries.

Certain fellow-communists and many adversaries have
written very critically about this line. Fellow-communists have
accused us of opportunism, of abandoning internationalism for
'nationalism'; of 'anti-Sovietism'; of desertion of a 'class
position': in a word, of something which has a connotation as
confusing as 'terrorist' — of *revisionism*. Articles and speeches by
leaders and functionaries of countries of the East which have
broadcast such accusations will be familiar to many readers.

On the other hand our political adversaries, and even some of
our allies, attack us or express reservations from another angle.
They say or hint that it may be a question of a plain 'opportunist
manoeuvre', on the one hand to facilitate an understanding with

other forces and emerge from the ghetto of an underground existence, on the other to achieve better electoral results and, in the long run, to open up a new road to government more easily for us, so that, once in government, from a position of strength, we can 'strike the blow and throw off the mask'.

In describing the criticisms from both sides, I am summarising; within them there are often more complex variations, but this is their meaning in essence.

Even though I regard them as profoundly erroneous – and in very many cases prejudiced and dishonest – I do not underestimate the effect of these criticisms, not only among certain working-class and popular strata, among professional people and intellectuals or members of the middle class, but also within our own party. Even in our ranks there may be those who consider we are verging on, if not actually entering the camp of the revisionists of Marxism, endangering our Marxist revolutionary concepts. And conversely, there may also be comrades who think that, in effect, our line is a sort of Machiavellism intended to raise us up at the right moment, above everyone else, and who regard this as a perfectly natural approach.

In everyday politics, even in a country like Spain, emerging painfully and uncertainly from forty years of dictatorship, the political parties – not ours – are resorting to all gimmicks which, tactically, will help them strengthen their position without bothering too much about principles. To these parties everything is forgiven and excused; their methods are accepted as legitimate since it is regarded as a matter of principle that, even if they win, they will not change the social system. Instead, general attention is focused on the communists; there is none of that tolerance for us. It is known that we propose to change the social system, for we make no secret of it. And many people fear that we might also irreversibly destroy political liberty and annul the rights of opposition, since other communist parties have done that in countries where they have triumphed.

But the roads we propose – the winning of a socialism which would maintain and enrich the democratic political liberties and human rights which are historic achievements of human progress that cannot be surrendered, and the imparting to them, furthermore, of a new economic and social dimension –

for the realisation of this ideal, it is not enough to rid ourselves of some of the formulas coined by our theorists, such as that of the *dictatorship of the proletariat*; or that we should affirm our respect for the democratic process. What is needed is a global analysis of modern developed capitalist society and its world context, as well as of the consequences of the advances in the means of production and the new social structures they have engendered. Of particular importance is the study of the modern State, especially the possibilities for its democratic transformation, and equally, a critical deepening of Marxist ideas.

Unless we work out a firmly-based conception of the possibility of democratising the capitalist State apparatus, thereby adapting it for building a socialist society, without its forcible total destruction, we shall either be accused of unscrupulous tactics or identified with social democracy.

For the State apparatus as a whole continues to be the instrument of the ruling class – an instrument that is greatly cherished. This is a Marxist truth. The State is not above classes; it is not an arbiter between them, as an ideology which goes back at least as far as Hegel – and which fascism carried to the extreme limit – endeavours to insist in one form or another. Without the transformation of the State apparatus, every socialist transformation is precarious and reversible, not by an electoral result which it would be logical and natural to accept, but by an armed coup carried out by the very people theoretically responsible for defending legality.

The Chilean experience shows that under the regime of Popular Unity, committed to a socialist experiment, the State apparatus continued to be an instrument of capitalist rule, deeply penetrated, furthermore, by US imperialism, its services and multi-nationals. This apparatus *overturned the whole process*, abolished the democratic constitution and established a savage military dictatorship when a favourable opportunity arose.

The capitalist State is a reality. What are its present characteristics? How can it be transformed? This is the problem of every revolution, including the one we propose to carry out by the democratic, multi-party, parliamentary road. It cannot be ignored.

Imperative, too, is a deeper study of the relationship between democracy and socialism, of the very concept of democracy which highly respectable Marxists have disposed of with what I, in my ignorance, regard as frivolity and haste.

It is equally worth reflecting once again, at this level, on the concept of socialism. We already have various examples of societies which have started out in one way or another along the road to socialism. Instead of making myths of them, above all in a period when religious myths are in crisis, we ought to study their experience so as to break away from the more or less prophetic and Utopian spirit in which our teachers approached the theme when they did not possess these experiences, so that we can obtain a better view of the various roads to socialism, their obstacles, their pitfalls, and even their limitations in certain conditions.

Again, when we look at things subjectively, from a fundamentally idealist position, we tend to forget basic elements of Marxism, such as the role of the development of the means of production, the level of which objectively influences the real content of the relations of production, regardless of our will.

The relations of production tell us the character of a society, of a social regime. But over and above the formal relations of production, the ultimate truth about their content lies also in the concrete development of the means of production, of the productive forces. Socialist relations of production which rest on an insufficiently-developed basis of the productive forces can only have *formal* socialist aspects, in the same sense as we refer to the *formal* freedom in bourgeois society. In other words, from the point of view of historical materialism, it is not enough to recognise the role of class struggle in social development – essential though this is. One must grasp the overall importance of the other dialectical component of historical materialism: the development of the means of production. There are occasions in history in which the tide of the class struggle permits momentary leaps that go further than the level of development of the means of production; but infallibly, in the course of time, this last factor recovers its weight and can overbalance, alter and jeopardise – up to a certain point – a leap forward made at the peak of the struggle.

The autonomy of the superstructure is real, within certain limits; but there is no such thing as its unlimited autonomy.

There are times when leaders who, from positions of power, think that the instruments of command, and their personal wishes or the wishes of those around them, can decide everything, overcome all obstacles and free them from objective laws, forgetting the determining factors to which the superstructure is subject. They proceed in fact like conspirators, needing at every step to find *scapegoats* who can be made to answer for the contrast between their plans and the actual possibilities. A similar error in reverse is committed by those critics – even well-intentioned ones – who seek to judge such mistakes and aberrations from a purely ethical standpoint. To approach these questions, on the contrary, in their true context in time in no way signifies the renunciation of revolution or of socialism. Nor is it – as far as I am concerned – the result of disappointment, or disillusion produced by the contrast between the Utopia, the myths that nourished us for a time, and the reality of what has been attained up to now by the revolutions and advances of the working-class and liberation movements. Today I believe in everything I believed in when I was twenty, and I have, essentially, the same dreams as I had then, I think with still better foundation. Those who have lost their dreams sadden and disappoint me.

With all its errors and aberrations, 'History' has progressed toward the point it has reached today thanks to those revolutions and advances. It is true that the historical process develops in the midst of great *anomalies*. Human will and the social sciences should play an ever greater part in overcoming and controlling the effects of these *anomalies*. But to deny the progress that has been made, to weaken, to allow oneself to be overcome by despair and disillusion, to stand on the sidelines assuming the role of a recorder of setbacks and a prophet of coming catastrophes, in no way befits a true revolutionary.

My respects to the aesthetes. They also can, and do, play a useful part in recording the limits beyond which politics should not go. They can be a sort of moral conscience. But if they themselves had to make policy they would end up on the gallows, in the clutches of the conservative forces, or deserting their posts to avoid risk. They would cause far greater catastrophes.

In saying all this, I do not want to deny that I have changed my way of looking at a series of questions, and that those who now and then remind me of this – or reproach me with it – are right. We communists have changed a number of viewpoints we held in other periods. Those who on occasion doubt the sincerity of these changes – people, many of whom have themselves fundamentally changed nothing at all and believe that we and the world, having completed a circle, are coming round to what have been their positions all along, without realising that the circle is not a circle but a kind of spiral which, while seeming to approach them, is rising and getting ever further away from them – these people are wrong. The natural tendency of a man, and particularly a man of character, pledged to a life-and-death cause, is 'Stick to your guns and don't yield an inch'. If we who cannot, I think, be denied character and firmness in our commitment to militancy, are amending it, it is because we have reached a profound conviction, in which personal and historical experience has played a decisive part. And what may perhaps be most valuable, is not that we ourselves have learned something and have the courage to say so, but that the testimony of our own lives is able to give us an authority which others, lacking the same experience, would not possess when the time came to change course.

There are many of us 'historical militants' of communism who have changed our way of judging a whole series of problems. I venture to say that with very rare exceptions we have all changed. And though it may seem a risky affirmation, I would add that those who have changed most are precisely those who do not appear to have changed at all, those who stubbornly go on repeating the formulas of thirty, forty, fifty and a hundred years ago. Because those formulas were then concepts whose reality was totally different from today's. They had an inner substance of revolutionary enthusiasm different from that of today. Those same words, those formulas, now refer to different, even contradictory, concepts; their real substance has in many cases become sterile and conservative. Although those who repeat them may be sincere and may not be aware that they have changed, they seem more like commonplace ministers of a religion stuck in officialdom than like revolutionaries fighting for a better world – not to mention those unworthy clerics who never do anything but carry out orders so as to maintain or improve their status in the hierarchy.

I am deeply convinced that those of us communists who have changed our way of looking at certain problems, who are striving to learn from experience, to grapple with concrete reality and deduce from it adequate guidelines for the struggle for socialism in today's world, are precisely those who at bottom have not changed – those of us who still feel ourselves responsible for the victory of socialism, unreservedly committed to the last breath to upholding the cause of communism.

In the history of the working-class movement there have been celebrated polemics – Engels against Dühring, Kautsky against Bernstein, Lenin against Kautsky, to mention the best-known – in which the term 'revisionism' acquired an ignominious connotation which some people are endeavouring to employ today against those of us who are modifying certain concepts, basing ourselves on the realities of our actual struggle and on the problems of the contemporary socialist movement.

But it is also forgotten that there was once a Marxist, revolutionary *revisionism*. Marx wrote in *The Eighteenth Brumaire of Louis Bonaparte*, with reference to bourgeois revolutions, that in these:

The tradition of all the dead generations weighs like a nightmare on the brain of the living. And just when they seem engaged in revolutionising themselves and things, in creating something that has never yet existed, precisely in such periods of revolutionary crisis they anxiously conjure up the spirits of the past to their service and borrow from them names, battle cries and costumes in order to present the new scene of world history in this time-honoured disguise and this borrowed language . . .

On the other hand [he added], proletarian revolutions, like those of the nineteenth century, criticise themselves constantly, interrupt themselves continuously in their own course, come back to the apparently accomplished in order to begin it afresh, deride with unmerciful thoroughness the inadequacies, weaknesses and paltrinesses of their first attempts (Marx/Engels, *Selected Works*, London, 1968, pp. 97–8).

That is to say, proletarian revolutions revise themselves, and revolutionaries do so too. Lenin *revised* certain theses of Marx and put forward the thesis of the *unequal development* of imperialism and the breaking of its weakest links to lay the foundation of the Great October Socialist Revolution. From the *formal* Marxist point of view Kautsky was right in affirming that in Russia the conditions did not exist for achieving socialism in 1917. The capitalist regime there had not reached a high level of development. But the *formal* Marxism of Kautsky could not be applied to the revolutionary crisis of Russia in 1917.

Lenin also *revised* himself on several occasions. The New Economic Policy adopted in 1919 *revised* the entire previous economic policy. When in his speech on the Chinese Revolution he spoke about the peasant Soviets, substitutes for the workers' Soviets in Russia, he was carrying out a revision of the Soviet experience, which took into consideration the concrete reality in China. When, on coming to power, he renounced the agrarian programme of the Bolshevik Party, to take over and make his own the programme of the Social-Revolutionary Party, was he not perhaps also revising?

Stalin, who claimed to be the successor of Lenin, calmly *revised* and annulled, with the approval of the appropriate authorities of the Communist Party of the Soviet Union, theses enunciated by Lenin. Khrushchev did not limit himself to revising; he condemned – rightly – practices and ideas of Stalin, with the approval of the 20th and 22nd Congresses. The present leaders of the Soviet Communist Party *revised* Khrushchev and furthermore buried him alive, politically speaking.

There is no need here to sort out what was just or unjust in these successive *revisions*, but one must conclude in the clearest and simplest form that *revision* – in opposing senses – has been undertaken not only by anti-Marxists but by the most outstanding Marxists. And that some of those who now tear their hair over the *revisionism* of the Communist Party of Spain and other Western parties, have been revisionists – even of their own work – on various occasions, though they may always have found scapegoats for actions for which, at least in one way or another, they themselves were responsible.

Today, to approach the problem of the democratic road to socialism, and the meaning of democracy, and the character and content of socialism as I do – solely on my own responsibility – in the following pages, means condemning ideas and solutions which I myself justified in other periods. In doing this, I am convinced that I, and all of us engaged in investigation along these lines, are remaining true to the essentials of revolutionary Marxism and upholding it. We are just as communist as we were in the past. We are not trying to 'hold out our hands' to decadent imperialist capitalism, but to speed up its abolition; we are not going over to the camp of social democracy, which we continue to combat ideologically. We want to act as Marxists, as communists, in the developed countries in which we are operating in the decade of the seventies.

The solutions we are putting forward will certainly not work for everyone; they are valid for our own and other countries at a similar or higher level of development. Those who demand pluralist and parliamentary development, for example, for Vietnam, Laos, and other regions of the Third World, where such institutions have never had any historical existence, are baying at the moon. Socialism and democracy will take on different forms in those countries. The same error, in reverse, is committed by those who want to set up their own models as *general laws* for revolution and socialism, and apply them to everyone else. Lenin's wise foresight regarding the different roads to socialism has been fully confirmed and even reinforced by reality.

Marxism is based on the concrete analysis of concrete reality. Either it is this or it is a pure *ideology* (in the pejorative sense of the term) which sets reality aside and is not Marxism; and the reality of the present day in Spain, Europe and the developed capitalist world has very concrete peculiarities which we cannot avoid. The conservative forces in Spain would be happier if they were faced with a dogmatic, sectarian Communist Party, adhering rigidly to outdated positions, which would continue to envisage the Spanish revolution as a simple replica of previous revolutions. Such a party would be supremely vulnerable, incapable of emerging from isolation and from the ghetto, or of making its mark on the political process and becoming a great revolutionary force, or of contributing towards and firmly establishing the hegemony of the working class in the life of the country. We are not going to give reaction that pleasure.

CHANGES IN THE STRUCTURE AND FUNCTIONS OF THE
STATE, FOLLOWING MARX, ENGELS AND LENIN

In essence, the attitude of Marx, Engels and Lenin towards the
State defines it as an instrument of the domination of one class
over others, stressing particularly its coercive character.

Other Marxists, among them Gramsci and Althusser, refer
also to the ideological apparatuses, which operate at the mental
level level rather than by violence. Among the ideological
apparatuses are the religious ones (the system of different
churches); the educational apparatus (the system of schools,
public and private); the family; the judicial apparatus; the
political apparatus; and the apparatuses of information (the
press, radio, television, etc.) and of culture.

To all this one should now add another dimension which the
capitalist State is increasingly assuming as representative of the
major dominant economic groups: the control of economic
development, which means that those parts of social activity
which escape the direct intervention of the State become
constantly more insignificant.

If the development of the productive forces shattered the
private, family character of production and provided it with
increasingly social forms which led to the continuous
development of the contradictions between the social forms and
the private, capitalist character of profit-making, the social
character of production today – of the service industries, of the
entire economy – has undergone a spectacular development as a
result of the intensive growth of the productive forces owing to
what is called the scientific and technological revolution.

The development of technology puts the very principle of
private enterprise in crisis, because only a few giants are in a
position to dispose of the immense sums of capital it requires.
The capitalist State steps in to make good private capital's
failures, using public funds to prop up those industries which
are unable to finance themselves or obtain sufficient private
credit. Together with the injection of capital, the same thing
happens with the reduction of charges for public services, the
lowering of taxes or the giving of export premiums. But when all
is said and done, the resources which the State deploys are those
of society. Without consultation, society as a whole supplies the

needs of capitalist development. In this way, the social character of the economy reaches colossal proportions. The least and humblest contributor is providing for monopolist concerns whose profit gets no further than their owners.

This role gives the capitalist State, as the instrument of monopoly capital, a decisive power of intervention in economic life.

Although the rulers still talk about liberalism and free competition, this latter, which really did exist in other periods of capitalist development, is totally disappearing. The fabulous growth of technology has killed it. And as the development of the class struggle has lagged behind the development of the productive forces, *it is not the socialist State that has put an end to free competition in our western world; it is the monopolists' state* which tries to assign itself a social function above classes and ideologies, in order to justify its continued existence.

One of the notable examples of the growing socialisation of the economy is shown by the decision of the French Government to give compensation amounting to some thousands of millions of francs to the farmers and stockbreeders hit by the serious drought of 1976. In former times, those of free competition, those social sectors would have had to meet natural calamities out of their own resources, seeking compensation for bad years in the good ones. Undoubtedly that system ruined the weaker farmers but, in conformity with its own logic, it acted in favour of the capitalist concentration of property. There would be no objection to the principle of solidarity from the whole of society with those who make the land produce – the principle invoked in the case of France. But what does deserve opposition is the fact that under State monopoly capitalism, the deterioration of the agricultural sectors is compensated for not out of the super-profit made by the great industrial enterprises, the banks and insurance companies, but from a lowering of the wages and salaries of the producers through taxation. Meanwhile, the big enterprises get their taxes reduced on the pretext of assisting their self-financing and the development of the economy. Besides, the distribution of compensation is in fact carried out arbitrarily, favouring the stronger crop farmers and stockbreeders and consequently stimulating capitalist concentration.

In the weaker capitalist countries, the State goes so far as to take direct charge of those enterprises and services which do not yield sufficient profit for private capital. Thus in Spain, through the National Industrial Institute (INI) and other official organisations, the State has largely taken over the steel industry, shipbuilding, the railways, etc.

Recently, according to some specialist publications, the INI has been taking over the property of some of the large multi-national enterprises which are leaving our country because the changes in the political situation lead them to have doubts about the future of their businesses.

The present-day State, which employs in its service not only the army, the police, the judiciary, the tax collectors and the traditional bureaucracy, but also hundreds of thousands of teachers, administrators, technicians, journalists and other workers, is still the instrument of class domination defined by Marx, Engels and Lenin; but its structures are far more complex, more contradictory, than those known to the three Marxist teachers, and its relations with society have quite different characteristics.

The socio-political system at the head of which this type of State is to be found, is that baptised with the name of 'neo-capitalist', which in the years of the 'fat kine' after the Second World War gave rise to all sorts of reformist illusions.

It was the period in which the development of consumption, the car, domestic electrical appliances, and the growth of the service industries, along with full employment, gave rise to an upsurge of all kinds of theories about the 'disappearance' of class differences and of the class struggle.

The French Professor Georges Burdeau, summing up some of these theories, spoke of a 'functional State', of a form of society 'whose fundamental tenets cannot be questioned since they correspond to the internal logic of social mechanisms', which 'invalidates the old opposition between capitalism and socialism, just as it resolves the antagonism between bourgeoisie and workers'; 'politics has no reason to try and change it [society]; its only task is to administer it, fitting in with its profound essence'.

The *profound essence* of this State, according to Professor Burdeau's summary, is '*the colonisation of the State by technology*', *'the despotism of technology,'* which dictates the State's objectives and takes problems out of the realm of politics to place them in the aseptic, classless and functional realm of the dictates of technological development.

These concepts are a distortion and a mystification of reality. In fact, the development of the productive forces has an enormous impact on the political and social system. That development poses new demands as regards the form in which the State is run. With the level of the productive forces as it exists today, the politics of society ought, in fact, to be concentrated on what Marx and Engels called *the administration of things.* But they related this attainment not only to the growth of technology but above all to the attainment of a society without oppressors and oppressed. And precisely what makes it impossible to take into account the 'dictates of technology' – and with its growth, the possibility of a new humanism in social relations – is the survival of these classes and the use of technology by the ruling class to try to maintain its domination and its privileges. In practice, what can really be inferred from the development of the forces of production is that modern society is ripe for socialism.

There is no room for doubt that the diversionist theories described by Professor Burdeau have been manipulated by the ruling economic groups, replacing the divine origin of power – in disuse today – by a new divinity, technology, which is shown as surrounded by the merits of the rational and the irrational at one and the same time. But to the extent that the period of the 'fat kine' has given way to one of 'lean kine', all these theories have been plunged into crisis. What seemed rational has ceased to be so, and the role of politics and of social contradictions has reappeared, dominating the pure 'dictates' of technology.

It has become evident that this new political Leviathan, even more monstrous than the one described by Hobbes, is today the centre of the countless contradictions affecting a society so tremendously vulnerable to all of them, and is – to extend the image, without in the least trying to minimise its power – a Colossus with feet of clay.

Despite its confused and anarchic features and its inconclusiveness, the movement of May-June 1968 in France did contribute towards exposing the signs of weakness in the

French State, behind its apparent omnipotence. That movement was, probably, the first great social revolt against this type of State – the precursor of other such revolts.

Though all the determining factors in the case are not yet clear, the Watergate scandal, in which certain ideological apparatuses of society entered into open conflict with the coercive apparatuses and won a victory over them, even though a limited one, is a confrontation characteristic of the contradictions that plague the present State system of monopoly capitalism.

Technological development, controlled by a small number of private groups, has raised the capitalist State to the zenith of its power, but at the same time to a high peak of crisis.

In the old days, the liberal bourgeois State presented the outward appearance of an *arbiter* State, which *mediated* between the opposing classes. When it intervened against the workers' protests, utilising brute force or class legislation, it did so in defence not only of one group of privileged capitalists but of all the other sectors and classes of society, of principles which were challenged only by the conscious proletarian minority.

CONFLICT BETWEEN SOCIETY AND THE MODERN STATE

Conversely, the State appears today, ever more clearly, as the *director* State in all spheres, particularly in that of the economy. And since it is the *director* State which no longer serves the interests of the whole of the bourgeoisie, but only of that part which controls the big monopolistic groups – economically fundamental but, humanly speaking, very small – it is now confronted, in its capacity as such a State, not only by the advanced proletariat but also directly by the broadest social classes and strata, including part of the bourgeoisie: it is entering into direct conflict with the greater part of society.

It is thus that in recent years, in the developed capitalist countries, we have experienced forms of social struggle, direct confrontations with the State apparatus, that we were not previously accustomed to, led by all kinds of farmers, traders and professional groups. We have also witnessed the emergence of forms of organisation of businessmen which, under various names – many of them using the word '*young*' more in the social sense than with regard to age – express the interests and viewpoints of the middle bourgeoisie, or else of sectors of what has been called the *technocracy*, buffeted by the contradictions between the social character of the organisation of the enterprises they manage and the fact that capitalist profit is the objective of those enterprises.

Thus vast social common interests are created, impossible in other times: between the consumer and the retailer against price policies; between the big farmers and the consumers; and between the working-class, the forces of culture, the peasants and bourgeois sectors. All these common interests occur against the great monopolist middlemen, or against the great monopolies which rob or exploit one or other of these groups, and in particular against the power of the State which appears as the definer and executor of economic management, which gives privileges to the few and harms the rest. The contradiction between the monopolist groups and the rest of society is embodied in the contradiction between the rest of society and the State power. From this moment on, it transpires that the political and social struggle which the *director State* or the *functional State* set out to suppress under the *dictates of technology*, now acquires a greater and more decisive importance and scope. Despite ineffectual neo-capitalist theories, the *State* is becoming less and less a *State for all* and more and more a *State for the few*. The struggle for State power becomes the centre of social preoccupation, and the capitalist system of the developed West, which appeared unchangeable and immune to all revolutionary threats, finds itself in fact facing a crisis which, even though it displays symptoms different from those of the social revolutions in the under-developed countries, is nonetheless a crisis with profoundly revolutionary prospects.

But a highly novel fact which a Marxist cannot dismiss by adopting static doctrinaire positions, a fact which he must confront with the Marxist method of *concrete analysis of the concrete situation* is that the contradiction between society and the State, given the present dimensions and features of the State apparatus, can and must culminate *in a crisis within that apparatus*, the members of which mostly have their origins in the underprivileged classes and are really in a similar class situation, and who, constituting as they do a mass force, cannot be separated off like the army and the police in barracks bristling with defences and isolated from the rest of society. It follows from this that the ideological and political currents which are developing in society have new possibilities of penetrating the State apparatus and of winning important sectors of it.

In spontaneous movements like that of May–June 1968 in France, society as a whole had not yet a clear understanding of this reality. But in subsequent years this understanding continued to grow, particularly in countries like France, Japan and Spain, and also, more slowly, in the metropolitan countries of what were once great empires, like Britain. The crisis, and together with it the thought-provoking actions of the vanguard forces, will undoubtedly lead to a more widespread and general understanding and to the clearer definition of the conflict between the great majority of society and the present powers of the State.

2

The Ideological Apparatuses
of the State*

That the structures of the present monopoly capitalist State are in a very shaky condition is demonstrated, in the first place, by the crisis of what Marxists call the ideological apparatuses of the State, of which it is important not to forget the *essential* role. When these ideological apparatuses are plunged into a crisis, the same crisis also affects the State coercive apparatus, whose members see the crumbling of the reasons which form the basis of their unshakeable and obedient loyalty to the aims dictated to them by the apparatus of authority.

In some revolutions of the past, the strategy of the forces of change consisted in condemning these ideological apparatuses *en bloc* and destroying them together with the repressive ones; but the vitality of the ideological apparatuses was shown in many cases to be infinitely stronger than that of the coercive ones. And while the latter were destroyed with relative ease, the former persisted, and the revolutions had to accommodate themselves and work out a compromise with them, sometimes extremely difficult, but necessary.

The strategy of the revolutions of today, in the developed capitalist countries, must be oriented to turning these ideological apparatuses round, to transform them and utilise them – if not wholly then partly –

---

* In this chapter I use the concept of 'ideological apparatuses of the State' and 'ideological apparatuses of society' without distinction, because some of these apparatuses still in fact preserve a certain autonomy in relation to the State, though this is steadily becoming less and less because the State itself is taking over an increasing number of functions.

against the State power of monopoly capitalism. Modern expérience
has shown that this is possible, and that this is the key – except in
the case of war or an economic and political catastrophe,
difficult to imagine today in the developed countries – to the
democratic transformation of the State apparatus.

This is not a matter of an abstraction, without any links
with reality; one need only take an unblinkered look at phenomena that are beginning to develop in front of our eyes, and
imagine their possible future development if we *intervene actively
in them*.

The oldest and most influential of the ideological apparatuses, the Church, finds itself today at the start of a crisis
probably more profound than the one which gave birth to
Lutheran Protestantism. That crisis was linked to the decline of
feudal society and the birth of the bourgeoisie; today's crisis is
linked to the decline of bourgeois society and the birth of
socialism.

On the one hand the advances of science and technology, and
the extension of culture to the broad masses, have overthrown a
series of dogmas and beliefs bolstered by infantile superstition
and widespread backwardness, which Lenin defined nearly sixty
years ago, when he wrote: 'The exploited . . . including those in
the most advanced and democratic bourgeois republics,
constitute, in their majority, a brutalised, uncultured, ignorant
and fear-ridden mass, lacking cohesion.' Lenin would not have
used these terms in speaking about the exploited masses of the
capitalist world today.

A new constellation of theologians, following the path
opened up by Teilhard de Chardin, aware of the inanity of a
whole series of formulas in which the 'faith of the simple' was
encapsulated, undertook a fundamental work of revision in
order to bridge the gulf which separated official Catholicism
from science. The myths of Adam and Eve, of the Creation, of
Heaven and Hell, and other myths, have been giving way to an
advanced Christianity more in keeping with the times. The
retreat and the growing isolation of integrist Catholicism are
clearly visible, above all after the Second Vatican Council,
though its remnants still have weight in the official Church and
particularly in Rome. The phenomenon known as the *aggiorna-
miento* (updating) has initiated in the Christian community what

can without exaggeration be regarded as a real cultural revolution.

As it could not fail to do, in the epoch in which socialism is beginning to be a reality, in which the existence of differentiation and class struggle covers the broadest sectors of society, this Christian opening towards science has had to go further, penetrating the social sphere, bringing a further opening towards the social currents of change, towards socialism.

In our country this evolution is clearly to be seen, more pronounced among the active members of the rank-and-file Christian organisations, but perceptible also in some sections (still much in a minority) of the Church hierarchy. The magazine *Posible* has made itself the echo of a confidential inquiry which the Spanish Episcopal Conference carried out among its bishops at the 24th Plenary Assembly, which met from 23 to 28 February 1976. To the first item in the questionnaire, on capitalism, the magazine sums up the replies as follows:

On Capitalism. Here the hierarchy burns its boats: capitalism is the negation of fundamental values, and little can be expected of it as it is resistant to reform. We select some of the most important replies:

Aspects of the capitalist system which contradict the Christian conception of life: All the replies agree in recognising that the four aspects indicated in the questionnaire (materialism, subordination of the individual to the economy, manipulation of freedom, and helplessness of the weak) exist under capitalism and are contrary to the Christian conception of life. Some add other aspects, for example: the desire for wealth as the ultimate root and motivation of all economic activity; the appropriation by capital of a great part of the fruits not only of capital but also of labour; the dynamics of competition, of struggle and confrontation in which it inevitably places people; the division into classes and the consequent social discrimination to which the system necessarily leads; a selfish concept of the common good; absolutisation of the right to private property, etc.

Several make the observation that the four aspects indicated in the questionnaire are also to be found in socialist systems with different nuances, and one reply maintains that these defects are not due to the structure itself but to the way it is used.

To the question: *Is it possible to cure the vices of capitalism through reforms?*, various replies affirm categorically that it is not possible because capitalism is rooted in a materialist philosophy and 'radically exploits man'. In addition, in the words of one answer, 'it does not appear possible ever to cure the *real* evils that spring from the nature of capitalism, and its concept of the relation between the forces of production and the distribution of profit . . .'.

Other replies state that it is possible, but add that it is very difficult. They point out the historical changes in capitalism, which under working-class pressure has softened and changed itself; but they point out that it must be recognised that capitalism seeks new forms of exploitation and certain of its innate evils continue unaffected.

Others recognise that the social doctrine of the Church has hitherto favoured capitalism through its concept of property rights, by its condemnations of the various forms of socialism and its lack of criticism of capitalism, and by presenting theology as the sanctifier of private property and obedience to authority. 'Certainly, worst of all is the fact that the Church, in the opinion of many, has allowed it to be thought that within its membership there can be a place only for those Christians – workers or employers – who have accepted the style and forms characteristic of the capitalist system.'

In its economic and social interests. All admit that the Church, in part and indirectly, favours the capitalist system in its own economic and social interest; that it is embedded in capitalist society and cannot disentangle itself from it. At times it has recourse to economic aid from the rich; it has deposits of 'securities' from foundations, etc.; at times it presents a face of luxury, etc.

In its silences: The majority of replies recognise that the Church has been too silent. Its performance of its teaching role has been inadequate and it has provided little teaching by oral instruction and preaching. It has made very few far-sighted or courageous proclamations.

The analysis of these replies definitely does not allow us to conclude that the bishops are inclining towards socialism. We are speaking of an ideological apparatus – the Church – in crisis, and not of one which has already turned into its opposite. According to the document in question, nearly all the bishops consider the choice of a non-Marxist socialism (presumably social-democratic) *legitimate* and some think it *very suitable*, although with near unanimity they reply that among the workers this choice is 'not accepted at all' since 'they do not regard it as a real alternative to capitalism'. 'It is no more than a variant of capitalism.'

The third question deals with the attitude towards Marxist socialism. Here the majority of the replies are negative as regards Marxism; a minority give more varied answers; some refer to the differences between the positions of one Marxist party and another, and recognise that there are those which 'sincerely respect democratic procedures, individual rights, and the right to criticise the socialist system itself, the rejection of violent methods, etc.'.

At all events, with the exception of one reply, all the rest affirm that a Christian 'can accept some elements of scientific Marxism' and all the replies admit that 'collaboration between Christians and Marxists for some specific objectives of a social or political type is permissible'.

Those who have read this article rightly stress the contradictions which run through it, and state that the bishops appear to be seeking a non-existent third road between capitalism and Marxism. Nevertheless, what seems most clear is that the top hierarchy has begun to doubt the viability of capitalism, without yet reaching logical conclusions – the recognition of socialism and consequently of Marxism as a solution – but approaching the problem without the threats of excommunication characteristic of the recent past.

Proceeding downward from the hierarchy, positions are opening more, as is shown by the existence of the 'Christians for Socialism' movement and the membership of Christians in the Communist Party and other Marxist groups.

It is known that, in recent years, in many seminaries, the students, helped in some cases by their teachers, have attentively studied Marxism along with theology, and in the practical experience of the class struggle in our country, churches and religious houses have served as refuges for workers' meetings. A Jesuit educational centre like the University of Deusto, for generations a hothouse for rearing cadres faithful to the system, has – at least to some extent – ceased to function in this capacity.

The crisis in the Church, as an ideological apparatus of capitalism, is a reality not only in Spain but also in a number of countries in Latin America and elsewhere, though the depth of the crisis varies.

In Italy itself, during the last legislative elections, a section of Catholics defied all the prohibitions of the Vatican and collaborated with the communists. It can be argued that this refers only to a minority who dared to disobey the Vatican, but this fact and the vote in favour of divorce in the famous referendum of 1975 are also indicative of the crisis.

While the Church has traditionally been the fundamental ideological apparatus of the ruling class and, as happened in Spain in the years 1936–9, when the Church supplied the Francoist uprising with its fundamental ideological basis, the crisis which is now developing within it may produce – and to some extent has already produced – political and social consequences of great importance not only among the broadest sections of the people, but also among those who make up the coercive apparatus of the State, who are accustomed to identify the defence of the State with the defence of the faith.

It should be stressed that the crisis of the Church as a capitalist ideological apparatus *does not necessarily signify a crisis in the Christian faith*. In certain cases it may point, on the contrary, to a kind of flowering of that faith. In coming nearer to Marxism, many Christians have revitalised their faith. We say that with the entry of Christians, our Party has gained a new dimension; one could perhaps add that the same has happened to the faith of our Christian members. The tasks connected with material life, with social transformation, with what our cause contains of redemption, fraternity and equality, bring back to the militant Christian the evangelical values, the purity, the generous devotion of the early Christians. We deeply respect these sentiments which, in those who are animated by them, free religion from the alienating character which the founders of Marxism attributed to it, and make it a stimulus for the liberation of mankind.

Is this crisis affecting the Church, which is opening cracks in its function as principal ideological apparatus of a class-divided society and changing one part of it into a factor for social transformation – a crisis more or less advanced in different countries – a transitory episode destined to fade away, to undergo a retrograde development? Is it a passing fever? Is it possible to base a new revolutionary strategy on it, a recovery of religious feeling for social transformation?

Unless there were some colossal catastrophe which would brutally plunge science and human progress back into the past, it can be said that this crisis, though it may not develop in a straight line, though it may have ups and downs, is part of an irreversible process.

The continuity of this process now depends not only on the Christians, or the spontaneous impact of social phenomena on the internal conflicts of the Church; it also depends a great deal on the understanding of the phenomenon by the revolutionary forces, and on the way they react to it.

It is not the simple repetition of doctrinal formulas valid in other periods, or, even less, an unpleasant after-taste of anti-clericalism that can help this process to advance and integrate Christians into the revolutionary forces. It is an understanding that the means of production, social change and the progress of science and culture in general have profoundly changed material structures and ideological superstructures; that, if the vanguard is conscious and acts accordingly, these changes are releasing, and can release even more powerful revolutionary forces which neither Marx, Engels nor Lenin could count on in their day.

If we make a broad evaluation of the role – decisive in the last resort – of the ideological apparatuses of the capitalist State, we must conclude that *turning them round*, not hindering but helping the processes that are going on, is a vital part of modern revolutionary strategy.

THE CRISIS OF THE IDEOLOGICAL APPARATUSES: EDUCATION; THE FAMILY

If the crisis within the Church can be clearly seen, no less clearly visible is the crisis in the schools, in the educational system as an ideological apparatus of the capitalist system.

There is no doubt that this has been induced by the end of education as the privilege of a small aristocracy, isolated from the people; by the spread of mass education as an imperative for technological development, and the fact that the extraordinary growth of the means of production objectively carries within itself – even before socialism – the tendency to sweep away the differences between manual and mental labour, even though the policy of the monopolies strives to maintain division between the skilled and unskilled sections of the working class.

Those who remember the universities and educational centres in the period before the Second World War, their methods, their teaching personnel, and their students, and who observe those centres today and the people who frequent them in one capacity or another, can appreciate the vast changes that have taken place.

Some of the most significant demonstrations of May–June 1968 in France – and we go back to this point of reference because in some measure, with all its confusion, it represents a kind of dividing line between two periods – took place precisely in the universities and centres of learning; they were an explosion of the crisis in the educational apparatus, a crisis which in Spain, under Francoism and under its heirs, has continued in full ferment.

It can be stated that *that moment in the institutes of higher education marked a great leap forward on the part of the forces of culture towards an awareness that in present day capitalist society their situation is essentially similar to that of the working class.*

Today the universities and educational centres do not merely inculcate bourgeois ideology: they frequently become centres of opposition to capitalist society. In fact, the whole educational system is in crisis. In several European countries, reforms are following one after another without resolving the essential problems.

The development of science and technology – save for a nuclear catastrophe – cannot be halted; it is equivalent to the development of the means of production. Formerly we Marxists thought that, when a certain ceiling was reached, the capitalist system would become an almost insurmountable obstacle to its own development. But practice has shown that, one way or another, the law of human progress breaks the strait-jacket of the social system. To maintain and reproduce itself, capitalism needs the development of the productive forces, even though this may be distorted by the laws of profit, giving rise to fresh conflicts and social contradictions. In the course of this, the universal extension of education is inevitable. The access of millions of young people to higher education deprives higher education of its character as an aristocratic stronghold, which it had in the years before the Second World War. Objectively, this adds an extremely important cultural contribution to the movement for change, broadening its horizons and its methods. On the other hand, the presence of hundreds of thousands – of millions – of young people in the universities, even though only a minority of them are of working-class origin, means that the majority belong to the middle and lower classes; that very many students have to combine study and work – often manual work; and that the university becomes a mirror of the conflicts existing in society, a focus where culture and science are studied in the midst of a constant debate on the problems of real life. Moreover, on leaving the lecture-halls the students now have to meet these problems, join the labour market and experience unemployment, whereas before when they joined a higher educational institution, they could count on a higher social position, in the State, in private enterprise, or in bourgeois politics.

Undoubtedly, the university should occupy a privileged place today in the activity of the revolutionary political forces. Not only because of its great concentration of masses of young people, available for action, but because in it are formed the cadres for the ideological apparatuses of society and because sowing the seed of Marxist and progressive ideas in their study-courses is one of the most effective means of ensuring that those apparatuses are *turned round*, at least partially. Capitalism needs the university as it needs the working class, but the university, like the working class, does not need capitalism. To such an extent is this true that a thoroughgoing reform, which would democratise education, raising its scientific level, its critical and pluralist character, and which would open it up to the great mass of young people, can only become a complete reality under a socialist regime.

Among the ideological apparatuses, the family itself, in its traditional sense, is in a period of profound transformation. The origin of this process does not lie in any voluntarist ideology. It begins as a consequence of the growing dehumanisation of life in the developed capitalist system, which throws the traditional concept of the family into a state of crisis. Then, when reality is recognised, a whole series of age-old rules and regulations start to collapse. Examples of this process are the progress – still far from sufficient – towards women's liberation by means of their economic independence in relation to men; the attainment of certain rights – even though many are still only formal – such as divorce, the use of contraceptives, abortion; the change from semi-patriarchal relations between parents and children to another kind of looser relationship in which children are more independent and freer in their thoughts and movements; lastly, the moral crisis directly affecting the family, beneath which is the search for a new morality in face of the breakdown of the rules which traditionally sustained it. In addition, a whole series of accompanying factors indicate that though the family, as a human nucleus, is not hurtling towards annihilation, it is in the process of transformation.

Does this mean that the family has changed to such an extent that today there is a rupture between it and the social system? Clearly, no. But the rupture of a series of traditional taboos does mean, for example, in a country like Spain, where tradition is still so strong, that the children of 'those who won the war' are politically confronting their parents, opposing their positions, and have even in quite a number of cases brought about certain concessions in parental attitudes. The children no longer obediently follow the family's ideological traditions, as they once did: they break with them, and even influence their parents.

If this can be clearly seen in Spain in the political field, it is also manifest – and not only in our own country – in the social sphere. In a number of groups in the middle strata, the social destiny of the children was previously traced out almost from their cradles and became part of the continuity of those same or similar strata, firmly fixed in the traditional system. Today's children have more opportunities and a tendency to choose their future more independently. The range of choice is still relatively narrow. But the family is ceasing to be the nucleus which almost automatically reproduces traditional social relations.

To sum up, it is not for nothing that we speak of a moral crisis in the capitalist West. This crisis is linked to the changes that have taken place in the economic structure, in the ideological apparatuses like those of religion and education, and in the repercussions of these changes on the institution of the family.

THE CRISIS OF THE IDEOLOGICAL APPARATUSES: THE LAW; POLITICS

As for the legal system, as an ideological and also a coercive apparatus, it is certain that the crisis is only beginning to make itself felt.

As long as there is no change of political power, the law will continue to justify and guarantee the forms of capitalist property. But already today, within the judiciary of countries like France, Italy, and Spain, in spite of the very fine sieve through which they are put when they are recruited, with the aim of ensuring their loyalty to the system, some sections – still a minority – are displaying attitudes which seriously question the independence of the judicial system – an idea that leads in practice to a conflict between justice and the existing State form, and which envisages substantial changes in procedure and the law in the direction of a new historic advance towards democracy. It can be predicted, in the absence of unforeseeable developments, that as the new students join the legal profession, this phenomenon will increase, and the opposition to traditional bourgeois justice will become more widespread. Moreover, this is so in a body which was a sanctuary of the most conservative groups, as much or even more than the armed forces themselves and the police.

To speak of the *political system* as an ideological apparatus, is not so much to refer to the constitutional pecularities of one regime or another – though these are not without importance – as to the set-up of political and social forces built around parties, trade unions, social movements, etc., on which the particular regime relies and which provide its defences.

To go back no further, let us examine the period between the Second World War and the present, confining ourselves to Europe. In this continent the capitalist system has been maintained on a framework which, in general, has extended on the right, from sectors such as that represented by 'Gaullism' in France, Christian Democracy in Germany and Italy, and other more traditional parties such as the British Conservatives or the Scandinavian right, to social democracy and the socialist parties on the left, with some additional parties of liberal tone towards the centre. This is obviously to set on one side the long-lived dictatorial regimes in Spain, Portugal, Greece and Turkey. In this equilibrium, in which the trade unions and mass movements with social-democratic leadership were integrated, capitalist development went on calmly, without great problems, in a period of great upsurge, without alternation of one group or another in power affecting the stability of the social regime.

This political system still appears to be strong in some countries in Central Europe and in Scandinavia, which are not so seriously affected by the economic crisis. Nevertheless, it is beginning to be eroded even there. The defeat of Olof Palme in Sweden and the social-democratic setback, together with the rupture of Christian Democracy in Federal Germany, are signs of this erosion. In fact, in these countries a certain, even though slight, retreat towards the right has taken place. It remains to be seen, however, whether this is any more than a simple adjustment to the internal balance of these countries' systems, or whether or not it will have repercussions in the internal processes taking place in social democracy, reinforcing its leftward or rightward tendencies. It is also very possible that the repercussions could be of one kind in Sweden and another in Germany.

In Britain, where the crisis is deeper, the instability of the system is also more pronounced. The Labour Party sees growing within it – as the recent (1976) Blackpool Congress has shown – left-wing tendencies which are demanding radical measures to nationalise the banks. Rejecting these demands, the Labour Prime Minister, Callaghan, countered with what he called the danger of an authoritarian regime. The growth of the Labour left and Callaghan's threats indicate that the health of the British political system, which has for so many years guaranteed capitalist stability in Britain, is problematic. For the moment this does not mean that the political system is threatened with a breakdown, but it is showing serious cracks.

The instability of the European political system is more serious on the southern flank of the continent. The downfall of the dictatorships in Portugal and Greece has taken place, and we are experiencing the up-hill march from dictatorship to democracy in Spain.

In Italy the political system of the *centre-left*, possible in the years of the 'fat kine', has exhausted itself. The left, and particularly the Communist Party, has achieved spectacular advances. The trade union movement has made serious progress towards unity. A new correlation of political and social forces, capable of gaining State power from the left, is taking shape.

In France, the political Union of the Left, parallel with trade union unity of action, is plunging the ruling political system into serious crisis, characterised during the period of the Fourth Republic by the collaboration between the centre and the socialists, and in the period of the Fifth Republic by the Gaullists, Giscardiens and other smaller groups. All the opinion polls agree that if there were elections today, the Union of the Left would win the majority of votes.

In short, it seems clear that the beginning of a breakdown of the equilibrium in the system of parties and organisations that have ensured the development of the capitalist system can occur today in the countries of Southern Europe, that a turn favourable to socialism can take place from now on.

The bloc of parties and organisations that has upheld capitalism in Western Europe has been receiving encouragement, support and directives from United States imperialism, which has assumed the leadership of the capitalist world. The anticommunist pressure of US diplomacy continues to be a factor making for distortion in the internal policy of certain European countries and is certainly a threat to democracy. It must not be forgotten that this pressure sustained Salazar and Caetano in Portugal, put the Greek Colonels in power, maintained Franco, and is now trying to deform the process towards democracy in Spain.

The United States is able to carry out this policy because the capitalist systems of Europe find themselves in a situation of dependence, to a greater or less degree, on American capital, through the weight of the multi-nationals and, in general, on the export of capital and the world monetary system, to which the dollar is the key.

The effects of this pressure sustain the Italian government on a Christian Democrat base, despite the situation of chronic crisis, and endeavour to promote a kind of European policy of *dissuasion* against the victory of the left in France.

In Western Europe today, United States imperialism and the

ruling social groups exert themselves to give credibility to the idea that *democracy equals capitalism* and, conversely, that *socialism equals Soviet domination.*

The trend which has widely been called 'Eurocommunism' must overcome this dilemma, and raise the question of democracy and socialism to the appropriate historic level. That is to say, it must demonstrate, on the one hand, that *democracy is not only not consubstantial with capitalism, but that its defence and development require the overthrow of that social system; that in the historical conditions of today, capitalism tends to reduce and in the end to destroy democracy, which is why democracy must proceed to a new dimension with a socialist regime.*

On the other hand, 'Eurocommunism' should demonstrate that *the victory of the socialist forces in the countries of Western Europe will not augment Soviet State power in the slightest, nor will it imply the spread of the Soviet model of a single party, but will be an independent experience, with a more evolved socialism that will have a positive influence on the democratic evolution of the kinds of socialism existing today.*

It is a question of a great ideological and political battle for democracy and socialism which should lead to the disintegration of capitalism's system of political relations, dominant today in Europe, and to a new correlation of forces favourable to social change.

In this respect, *the independence of the communist parties in relation to the Soviet State and other socialist States is essential, as is the theoretical and practical definition of an unequivocal democratic road.*

It is also essential to link the destiny of the working class with that of the broadest non-monopolist social classes. *The socialist revolution is no longer a necessity only for the proletariat, but for the immense majority of the population as well.* In these conditions, the idea of the alliance of the forces of labour and culture, of the new historic bloc and, in general, the question of anti-monopolist alliances, acquires decisive importance.

The system of political and trade union forces which has upheld the capitalist regime in Europe during these decades cannot be transformed by violence; it is also an ideological system which had, and still has, great mass support. In France the Socialist Party has profoundly changed its policy and has brought about the Unity of the Left with the Communist Party.

Monopoly capital in our neighbour country finds itself in an unstable situation not only because of the crisis, but because of this change in the Socialist Party which prevents monopoly capital from relying on a weapon which was essential for its equilibrium. In Italy, where the socialists did not make this change in time, they have lost ground and are very much shaken, whereas the Communist Party won the greatest electoral success registered by a communist party in the history of the West.

The crisis also affects the Christian forces.

In present conditions, the only way towards changing the ideological-political apparatus which upholds the capitalist regime is *the creation of a new correlation of forces by means of political, social and cultural struggle.* This new correlation requires the encouragement and strengthening of sincerely socialist positions within the socialist and social-democratic parties, and of progressive currents in the Christian movement. It is with these sectors that the communist parties can create a new system of political forces that may withdraw the mass support which today upholds monopoly capital, and could be the basis for a democratic march to socialism.

In speaking of political, social and cultural struggle, we bear in mind, in the first place, the value of the direct experience of the broadest masses in the struggle for their specific interests and for genuine participation in social decisions, to guarantee their defence. For this reason it becomes essential to promote action by the working class and the sectors affected by monopoly capitalism, to achieve the linking-up of these actions, to raise the people's ability to understand the global character of each other's struggles, overcoming narrowness of outlook, sectionalism, and the parish pump approach, and to bring together the economic, cultural, social and other demands with the demand for an ever more profound democratisation of society. In this way, the struggle for socialism is closely linked to the struggle for more democracy.

With this prospect, the working class, the advanced forces of culture, and specifically we communists, must get used to speaking on behalf of the majority of society, not only in words but in our very concepts. That is to say *we must think out, we must take up* the global problems of society. This is the precondition for assuming a hegemonic role.

In this sphere the parties of the bourgeoisie usually have the advantage over us. From the time of the bourgeois revolutions or transformations, the bourgeoisie has been accustomed to speak as the representative of society. At one time, when it was a progressive class, it had grounds for assuming that role. It no longer has any. Today it has set apart an oligarchy which actually represents the interests of no more than a tiny social minority – which dominates the State. Nevertheless, the parties manipulated by the oligarchy continue to speak in the name of society and present themselves as the protagonists of all human progress. They regard themselves as the authors of the development of the productive forces which, on the contrary, are derived from tendencies and social laws which operate at times in spite of them. They regard themselves as the authors of all the political and social progress that has been achieved by the masses, usually in struggle against them and in opposition to their own powers. But skilfully, through the fact of having been in power, and even though in general they have acted as a brake, these parties attribute to themselves the successes, and the more backward sectors of the population end up by believing them.

On the other hand, the forces of change and revolution always tend to speak in the name of one class, the proletariat, which with the forces of culture has certainly been the motive force of all progress, and which constitutes the essential pivot of all action for change.

At times they speak of a proletariat which is not the one that really exists, with its differing levels of development, some advanced and others backward, but a mythical, fictional proletariat, a bloc fully conscious of its historic mission which, at the end of the tale, becomes a sort of metaphysical, inoperative finger of God. But they must – we must – learn to speak on behalf of the vast majority of society, in the name of the nation, which means bringing together the actions of the advanced forces of labour and culture with the interests of the broadest social groupings, consciously taking up their defence, with the mission of representing the vital forces of the nation. Moreover, this must be done, as much in the social and political sphere as in that of ideology and culture, displacing the parties controlled by the oligarchy and the 'saviours' it puts forward at moments of crisis in order to manipulate and divert the people's desire for change.

THE CRISIS OF THE IDEOLOGICAL APPARATUSES: THE COMMUNICATION MEDIA

Among the ideological apparatuses of the State and of modern capitalist society are the communication media: television, radio and – to a lesser extent – the press. These are certainly the ideological weapons most to be feared today, because they penetrate into every home, sometimes in aggressive form, sometimes insidiously; in some cases on an openly political level, in others through the presentation of current affairs, and even in advertising, performing an alienating, brutalising role. In the capitalist countries, generally speaking, the media today are the most dangerous *opium of the people*. Nevertheless, in countries where the democratic movement is strong and broadly implanted in the cultural field, it is possible at times to utilise the media, even if only to a minimum extent, for progressive purposes. Unfortunately, this is not yet the case in Spain.

It is clear that a radical change in the use of these powerful instruments is impossible without a change of political power. But the struggle for the democratic control of the media such as television and radio, in such a way that the various forces of society, and not only the rulers, may find expression through them; the drawing up of laws to guarantee genuine press freedom – that is to say, the *material* possibility for all the great political and social forces to possess their own organs of expression, which goes much further than the freedom of the press, although it is not incompatible with it: these are steps which can enable the forces of change to undertake a struggle from within what today are ideological apparatuses of society.

From this point of view, the action of the revolutionary and progressive forces to carry their hegemony into the sphere of culture becomes essential. The precondition for this is the struggle for *genuine freedom of culture*. Only in conditions in which culture is free can these forces win hegemony. When the creators – whether scientific, technical, literary or artistic – are not free, culture withers, becomes crippled, changes into a camp of extreme conservatism, and this happens whatever the political or social regime. A flourishing culture does not tolerate prohibitions, and the flowering and extension of culture is the sphere in which revolutionary and progressive ideas can establish themselves, become hegemonic and have even more influence in the march of humanity, penetrating and transforming the ideological apparatuses.

THE STRUGGLE FOR THE CONTROL OF THE IDEOLOGICAL APPARATUSES

The problem which we must tackle is, in substance, *the struggle to win positions, dominating as far as possible, for revolutionary ideas in what are today the ideological apparatuses of society*, those on which the authority and moral and material force of the capitalist state are based; and this as much in the Church as in education, culture, the system of relationships among political forces, the information media, etc.

This does not mean winning these positions for one party, but for all revolutionary and progressive forces, which should increasingly identify themselves with democracy. Going beyond Gramsci's idea of the organic intellectual, and emphasising the possibilities which the strategy of the alliance of the forces of labour and culture offers the working class, is the idea of the new historic bloc. It is realistic to think of developing within these ideological apparatuses a struggle, *to turn them*, partially at least, against what was their original aim.

In the days of Marx and Engels, and even in those of Lenin, this perspective could have been dubbed utopian. It seemed more logical, therefore, to destroy these ideological apparatuses, along with the whole bourgeois State apparatus, by violent overthrow, and to replace them radically by ideological apparatuses created by the new State power. However, later on, practice showed that it is easier to create new apparatuses of coercion than it is to create ideological ones, and that the old ideology continued to circulate, in many instances, within these, impregnated, although in another direction, with metaphysical essences designed to idealise the new order and to stifle criticism.

But what was utopian at the time of Marx and Engels is no longer so today. For while the proletariat continues to be the main revolutionary class, it is no longer the only one; other strata, other social categories are placing themselves objectively within the socialist perspective and are creating a new situation. This is not an abstract theoretical idea, but a practical observation.

The crisis of the capitalist system, which is appearing in all areas, not only in economics and politics but conclusively in the cultural and moral – in other words, the ideological – spheres as well, is on the one hand a result of these changes, and on the other a factor which favours and accelerates them.

Even Althusser, who can at times be reproached for acting like the rigid and jealous guardian of the texts of Holy Writ, recognises in his essay 'Ideology and Ideological State Apparatuses (ISAs)' that:

The class (or class alliance) in power cannot lay down the law in the ISAs as easily as it can in the (repressive) State apparatus, not only because the former ruling classes are able to retain strong positions there for a long time, but also because the resistance of the exploited classes is able to find means and occasions to express itself there, either by the utilization of their contradictions, or by conquering combat positions in them in struggle (*Lenin and Philosophy and Other Essays*, London, 1971, p. 140).

And in a footnote Althusser adds:

But the class struggle *extends far beyond* these forms, and it is because it extends beyond them that the struggle of the exploited classes may also be exercised in the forms of the ISAs, and thus turn the weapon of ideology against the classes in power (ibid.).

Certainly one of the great historical tasks of the present time for the conquest of state power by the socialist forces is the determined, resolute, intelligent struggle to *turn the weapon of ideology, the ideological apparatuses, against the classes which are in power.*

DEVELOPED CAPITALISM AS THE BEARER OF SOCIALISM

It has become possible to propose this road because 'material upheavals' have taken place in the conditions of economic production with truly extraordinary changes in the structures and social relations in recent decades, all of which have ripened the conditions for socialism. If Lenin could say in 1917 that capitalism in its imperialist form was the ante-room to socialism, this is even more evident in the seventies.

Within the State monopoly capitalism of today something is already stirring which is more than the foetus of the new society, striving to break out, to emerge into the open.

The reformists have given the name of *socialism* to a whole collection of structural changes and measures of social policy which have been carried out in the developed capitalist countries. It is clear that there has been a falsification of the concept of *socialism*, since the capitalist system continues to exist.

However, we communists, obsessed by the qualitative change represented by the taking of power, have sometimes underestimated the gradual modifications which the system has been undergoing which are objectively beginning to break down its structure. These material upheavals could be summed up as follows:

1. The extraordinary development of the productive forces; the fact that education is more integrated to production, with the raising of the quality of the work-force; the development of energy, with the conquest of nuclear power and the discovery of new sources of energy; and the development of technology in general – a fundamental factor in all the changes of the period, in accordance with historical materialism.

There is no doubt that this development is already being held back by the capitalist system. With a world socialist system, productive forces could be used to their full extent in the sphere of peaceful production – productive forces capable of putting an end to hunger and want in the whole world and helping the underdeveloped countries rapidly to overcome their historical backwardness.

In reality, the enormous military expenditures, totally unproductive, are in themselves an obstacle to all this progress, and a squandering of wealth which may perhaps have affected the cycle of economic crises – displacing their destructive effects – and above all reducing their intensity, until recently when the crisis of the system, acquiring new characteristics, has broken all bounds.

2. The inability of the system of private enterprise to administer and channel the torrent of productive forces, even with its new multinational dimension. Today, the multinational

enterprise relies on the credits and various loans provided for it by the States of those countries where it is installed, which extract them from public funds and savings. Consequently, the essential role of the State and of society is all the more visible in the creation and maintenance of these enterprises, which continue to be, in defiance of all logic, private property. Hence the conditions for a socialist economy have matured.

The idea of an economy guided by a world plan is an intrinsically socialist idea. With truly prophetic vision, Gramsci wrote:

Before the conditions are formed for an economy directed by a world plan, it is necessary to go through a series of multiple phases in which the regional combinations (of groups of nations) may be many and various.

In the present period, the internationalisation of the productive forces has forced the capitalist regimes to find forms of regionalisation, that is to say, social forms of extra-national scope like the Common Market, and if they are constantly threatened, this is due above all to the contradiction between the social form and the private nature of the appropriation of profit. Hence the justification of the prospect of a Europe of the peoples, a socialist Europe, which is the social form under which Europe could become a reality in all aspects.

3. The assumption by the State of social functions which are a poor imitation of collective solutions: some public services, some enterprises, social security, health, education, compensation for social groups at risk (such as support for farm prices within the Common Market) – all measures which the capitalist State finds itself obliged to take in order to avoid the imbalance and the serious social conflicts which could be engendered by their neglect, and which enable the capitalist State to maintain the predominance of the monopolist oligarchy under the appearance of a *welfare state*, but which at the same time sharpen the contradiction between State and society.

Undoubtedly the crisis, as it sharpened, could lead that State to do away with many of the 'welfare' aspects so as to guarantee the profits of the oligarchy. But this would not be possible without resorting to open forms of dictatorship, to the abolition of democratic freedoms. This is a tendency which may develop, though it would not now be easy to enforce its acceptance.

4. The sharpening of the differences between the oligarchic minority and the rest of society and – to use a classical, though perhaps in the 'consumer society', a confusing term – the proletarianisation of professional people, in the sense of the unifying of their social position (although in many, but not all, cases their earnings are greater) with that of the wage workers. In addition, the introduction of forms of cooperation, though minimal, in the countryside, in order to resist the capitalist concentration of ownership; and the ever-increasing difference between oligopolist interests and those of small and medium enterprises.

To sum up: the development of conditions for a new correlation of forces favourable to socialism, creating the possibility of winning and consolidating it democratically, without recourse to forms of dictatorship.

5. The greater independence in the policy of the former colonies, which, by revaluing oil and other raw materials, are in a position to reduce and even cancel the super-profits taken from them by colonialism and neo-colonialism – profits which allowed, and to some extent still allow, monopoly capitalism in the developed countries to keep broad social sectors in its orbit, thus propping it up. This greater independence has had a decisive influence in the present crisis and operates objectively, though amid tensions, in favour of a greater democratisation of international relations.

Just as bourgeois society was formed in the womb of the feudal regime, so socialist society has matured in the womb of developed capitalist society. This is what gives us today a material base for setting ourselves the task of turning the ideological apparatuses on which the State relies against the present class society.

3

The Coercive Apparatuses of the State

NO CLASS CAN MAINTAIN STATE POWER IF IT LOSES HEGEMONY IN THE IDEOLOGICAL APPARATUSES

Certainly the ideological apparatuses are not everything in capitalist society and the capitalist State. There remain the coercive apparatuses, the apparatuses of force. But Althusser, in the essay mentioned above, says, correctly in my opinion:

> So far as we know, no class can maintain state power in a lasting form without exercising at the same time its hegemony over and within the State ideological apparatuses.

To give a correct reply to the form of solving the problem of State power here and now, it must be asked: Is it realistic in the developed capitalist countries to envisage the first step of the socialist revolution as the destruction by an act of violence of the coercive apparatuses of the State?

The question could be put in these terms in Tsarist Russia, in a situation of catastrophic military defeat, when the entire State apparatus had crumbled, and a great part of the army, desperate for peace, bread and land, and humiliated by the disaster, went over to the side of the revolutionary forces; and when, in addition, the memory was still alive of another defeat, at the hands of the Japanese navy, and incompetence and corruption were proverbial.

Radek, in his essay 'The Evolution of Socialism from Science to Action', writes:

> The theoretical propaganda of the revolutionary social-democrats [in

other words the Communist Party], and the blows which capital had
inflicted daily on the proletariat since the end of the last century, were
not together enough to lift the growing agitation of the proletariat
beyond limited attacks on capital. . . . So there arrived, at long last,
the monster of the long-awaited world war, which began to preach to
the proletariat with guns the doctrines it had not understood when
preached by revolutionary socialism.

The Russian Revolution is the first response by the proletariat to the
world war.

The establishment of socialist regimes in Eastern Europe was
also linked with war – with the Second World War, and with the
defeat of fascism in that war. In the same way, the victory of the
socialist revolution in China is an event closely related to the war
against Japanese invasion and to the world war against fascism.

Other revolutions have subsequently triumphed by arms, it is
true; but this has been in the form of national wars against a
foreign invader or against colonial powers, sparked off by the
results of the Second World War. The sole exception, perhaps, is
Cuba, a real surprise of history which up to now it has not been
possible to repeat in any country of the American continent.
With all this, it must not be forgotten that the victory of the 26th
July Movement, right under the nose of US imperialism, was
possible because that movement was not a socialist party but a
kind of national front which later, as the revolution advanced,
divided up, and in which the powerful personality of Fidel
Castro and his closest collaborators produced a later turn
towards socialism, while the right-wing section went over
openly to the American camp.

Would it be revolutionary and realistic today to predict the
passage to socialism in the developed capitalist countries as a
response by the proletariat to a third world war? If we are now
experiencing the longest period without a war in Europe in this
century, this is largely due to *dissuasion by terror* and not to
imperialism having lost its rapacious character; the proof is that
there are still local wars in the countries of the Third World,
where the risk of nuclear weapons being used is more remote.
But today, in Europe, a war would be nuclear and very quick,
and when it had ended there would be no social classes left to
dispute the leadership. In the first paragraphs of the *Communist
Manifesto*, Marx and Engels, referring to the fact that the

(written) history of mankind up to our day is the history of class struggles, stated that this struggle 'has each time ended either in a revolutionary re-constitution of society at large or *in the common ruin of the contending classes'*.

A war in Europe, which would at the same time be a world war, would end in such a ruin of the contending classes, because it would bring with it the virtual destruction of mankind and its material and social achievements.

Engels already indicated that the forms of waging war also influenced the waging of the class struggle, and that was at a time when nuclear weapons had not even been dreamed of. To ignore this factor and to continue to talk about the revolution with the same ideas as in the past – even the recent past – is no longer revolutionary.

Certainly the possibility cannot be excluded that in a favourable international context, in a developed country, in which there was no freedom and the ruling class exercised a brutal dictatorship against the people, a revolution might triumph by an act of force, providing the people won the support of a decisive proportion of the armed forces. But even in such a case, if the victory were not won very rapidly, if the country were plunged into a long civil war, in which the great powers were to become involved, the consequences might be catastrophic.

Without entirely excluding this possibility, it is clear that the roads to socialism in countries of the kind we are speaking of have to be different, taking concrete reality into account. They have to be roads in which democratic mass action is combined with action by the representative democratic institutions; that is to say, by the use in the service of socialism of the representative democratic instruments which today basically serve capitalism.

HOW CAN THE STATE APPARATUS BE DEMOCRATICALLY TRANSFORMED?

With this prospect in view, the problem is not only how to attain government. It is – and will be – *how to transform the State apparatus*.

I have already spoken about the State ideological apparatuses, about the possibility – the necessity – of developing a struggle in the various spheres in order to turn them round so as to oppose them to capitalism. Now it becomes a question of seeing how a turn of this kind can help to transform the coercive apparatuses, the last resort of capitalist State power.

The way, even within existing society, even before socialist forces enter government, is through energetic and intelligent action for the democratisation of the State apparatus. The starting point lies precisely in obtaining a situation in·which bourgeois ideology loses its hegemony over the ideological apparatuses.

To the extent that this objective is achieved, even partially, the results will be reflected in the coercive apparatus.

In this respect, May 1968 in France was an interesting experience. At the outset the forces of public order operated with brutality; but in the course of the struggle, these forces resisted their being used by authority as a repressive instrument against the people. A series of stands was taken in the professional police unions which protested against being used by the authorities and showed a wish not to confront the people. Some moments of wavering also occurred within the army.

Perhaps the reason why these tendencies did not go further was that, at that time, there was no real alternative power facing the established power. The left was disunited. I think it is not unjust to say that the political forces representing it were taken by surprise by the magnitude of the crisis and were not ready to overcome the disunity and lack of preparation in the short time during which the disturbance of the established power lasted.

At the same time, the new characteristics of that crisis, which could not be resolved by street action alone, or by a frontal attack against authority as in other classic crises, required various democratic initiatives, including new elections, to support the mass struggle with a serious and responsible alternative such as that offered today by the Union of the Left. The lack of such initiatives facilitated the action and the excessive weight of immature, anarchistic groups, which intimidated broad sections of the middle strata as well as the State apparatus itself, and reduced the influence of the left which had for a moment been so high among the masses.

This enabled the authorities, after weeks of impotence, to regain the political initiative and to benefit from the holding of elections.

The left had given too resounding a demonstration of its strength, and at the same time its unpreparedness and incoherence, not to provoke a reaction, which was cunningly exploited by the Gaullist authorities. And if that reaction was not able to go further, it was certainly due to the responsible example set by the working class.

Nevertheless, May 1968 helped to prepare the conditions for the future triumph of the left in France. It also created in the forces of public order, and probably among the armed forces, also shaken by the Vietnamese and Algerian experiences, a state of mind which already represented the beginning of a change in their attitude towards the problems of society and their role in it.

Recently, on the occasion of the workers' actions against the austerity plan of Raymond Barre and President Giscard, the Paris police took part in those actions with noteworthy demonstrations, and a debate developed in their trade union in which their role in society was again questioned.

In the French army, too, interesting events are occurring, not only at the level of the private soldier, but even among senior officers. Among the latter, there is dissension in the professional field about military doctrine; however, this is not surprising because it is logical in such circles for political and social contradictions to express themselves as conflicts in this area.

Without exaggerating their importance, these are phenomena unimaginable in the days of Marx and Engels and only conceivable in Lenin's day under other forms, in a crisis such as that of 1917.

It seems that in Italy, too, the effects of the crisis of the ideological apparatuses and those of the development of class struggle in a variety of spheres are beginning to be felt inside the coercive apparatuses of the State. Recent elections in Rome, for instance, seem to confirm that a substantial section of the forces of public order voted for the Italian Communist Party. Also significant are the events taking place in the judicial apparatus, several of whose personnel have been attacked by fascist terrorists.

In some of the armies of NATO, for example the Dutch, trade union organisations, which include officers and other ranks, are functioning. Military commentators declared that in the joint manœuvres this did not prevent the Dutch army from efficiently fulfilling the missions entrusted to it. But could such an army be used for a coup d'état?

Furthermore, in the developed capitalist countries, generally speaking, the entry of the civil servants into trade unions is a fact, and the functionaries, regarding themselves as a part of the public service, are tending more and more towards an employer/employee relationship with the State that pays them.

In other words, those who form the State apparatus – for the moment we are speaking only about a tendency – are becoming aware that authority uses them in many cases against the interests of society; they are beginning to recognise the contradictions between society, which goes one way, and the State, which goes another, and to regard the State power as an arbitrary *boss*. They do not do this out of narrow professional interests, or of those of their own particular group, but from a clearer and more consistent conception of their relation to real society, a relationship which the monopoly capitalist State deforms and manipulates for its own ends.

That is to say, parallel with developments in society as a whole, those who make up that enormous enterprise which is the modern State, are becoming conscious of the growing divorce between State power and existing society, of which the civil service officials are part.

This is of course a process which is only beginning, is therefore only incipient, and could still be diverted and manipulated by the ruling classes. It is an open question that has not been solved. It is a possible road for proceeding to the democratisation of the State apparatus as the first step towards its transformation and conversion into one capable of serving a democratic and socialist society.

THE STRUGGLE FOR THE DEMOCRATISATION OF THE STATE APPARATUS

In order to open this road, the Communist Party and other parties that stand for socialism, the whole of society's forces of change, must adopt a different attitude towards the State apparatus – coercive or non-coercive – from the one they have historically maintained.

The practice of class struggle has led to a confrontation

between the working people and those who make up these apparatuses. When there is a demonstration or a strike, it is not the managers of Banesto or Altos Hornos (two large Spanish companies) in Spain, or of the Banque de Paris or the leaders of Dassault in France – and so on, in other countries – who go on to the streets and physically confront the strikers and demonstrators; it is the forces of order, the police and, in extreme cases, the army. It is this role, which the State power of monopoly capital makes the armed forces play, that must be opposed.

The forces of public order, the police, should exist to defend society from anti-social elements, to control traffic, to protect the population. Popular demonstrations and strikes are not conflicts of public order, except when governments launch the police against them. Strikes are a matter for negotiation between employers' and workers' representatives. The preservation of order at demonstrations should be carried out by the demonstration organisers.

Modern society would be more secure if the police concentrated on the pursuit of theft and crime, and on tracking down anti-social elements who traffic in drugs; if they defended society against increasing gang aggression; and if they patrolled the roads more effectively to prevent the many fatal accidents; and if, in general, the police were in closer contact with the population and its problems.

Why put thousands of police in Martian uniforms to attack strikers and popular demonstrations with modern repressive equipment? Let the rulers get used to seeing demonstrations with legitimate demands, and to receiving the delegations appointed to negotiate with them. Let them get used to holding dialogues with the people, to listening to them, and even to rectifying their own decisions. Let authority not regard itself as being above society!

Employers should negotiate directly with the workers. Let them stop arrogantly thinking they can impose their *diktats* with the support of the police. If in a particular case they are unable to grant what is demanded, let them prove this to the workers, through a system of negotiation which lets the workers know, clearly and at all times, the financial position of the enterprise; this, in addition, would be a decisive means of putting a stop to

tax fraud. It very often costs society as a whole more to maintain
and mobilise the special units for intervention on the employers'
behalf than it would to grant the thoroughly legitimate
demands of the workers.

That is to say, it is a question of struggling, by political and
ideological means, with the aim of establishing a new
conception of public order, a more civilised one, based on the
idea of the defence of the entire population and not just the
interests of a privileged minority; a new conception of a more
democratic public order, and of instilling this conception into
the minds of those who make up the forces of order. These
forces, too, to a great extent, feel increasingly uneasy with the
tasks imposed on them by the present system.

They complain that the public judges them by the negative
aspects of their service and not by its positive aspects; they feel
themselves surrounded by public apathy, obliged to perform
tasks which lower their morale; and to do this against social
groups acting for interests which are also their own. For if the
cost of living is increasing, if health and education are not
available to everyone, if the social services are inadequate, the
families of the forces of order certainly suffer like all other wage-
earners.

Why should public order consist in defending the authority of
a government or a ministry which acts capriciously? Why should
it consist in defending a government, and not society?

Nor does public order mean the all-out defence of a
particular socio-political system, of particular institutions. If
the majority of the population is not in agreement with this
system, or with certain of its institutions, and declares against
them, then the defence of public order means guaranteeing that
that will of the majority is carried out.

A policy of the democratisation of the forces of public order
must be devised in accordance with the particular circumstances. A primary condition is that those who belong to those
forces should be allowed to unionise themselves in order
to defend their rights and their professional dignity, and to
establish relations with the working people which are not those
between policeman and suspect.

Those proposing to transform society should start a
continuous public debate on the role of the forces of public

order in a democratic society; they should take an interest in the material, social and professional problems of this sector. It is a difficult change to make. But it must be made, starting from the principle that in a democratic socialist society it will still be necessary to have functionaries who are specialists in the pursuit of crime, and in safeguarding the security of the population.

This does not constitute an obstacle to the denunciation of groups which specialise in repression directed against the people, or to the struggle for their elimination or conversion, according to circumstances. But with a correct policy, allies can be found in the public forces themselves against such groups, which are often those who discredit the profession as a whole. In the present situation of social crisis, a correct policy can in this respect help to win an important part of the forces of public order for democracy.

The army is, without doubt, the most important of the coercive instruments of the State. Various experiences, among them that of Chile in 1973 – and many others – prove that in some conditions the army can become the *political party* of the oligarchy: a political party with aircraft, tanks, artillery, machine-guns and rifles, which the oligarchy throws on to the scales when universal suffrage threatens its privileges. Moreover, the army has generally been formed ideologically in colonial and imperialist wars and in repressive actions against the people. Correspondingly, a part of the cadres of the armed forces came, not long ago, from the nobility and top bourgeoisie, and upheld the principle of identifying *the country with the political and social system.* The sincerely motivated patriotism of the officers was the ideological reflection of a class, anti-popular structure. This type of patriotism identified itself with order, not simply public order, but order insofar as it safeguarded the established social system. The concept of discipline was the reflection of the subordination of the ruled to the ruling classes in society; the idea of service to one's country contained within it that of service to an established power.

Automatically, these ideological reflections led the main nuclei in command of the armed forces to oppose all political and social change, since they identified the existing state of things with country, order, discipline, service.

Hence there arose, conversely, the anti-militarist traditions of the left, the historical lack of confidence shown by the masses in the army, and the fact that the revolutionary forces wrote the destruction of the army into their programmes.

However, the traditional concept of the army has gradually entered a crisis. The two world wars have contributed to this; in them not only the armies but the officer corps had to be opened, at least temporarily, because of the terrible slaughter. The great battles created a hint, if not of democracy, of a less class-ridden atmosphere in the military structures. Following the First World War, this did not change the dominant ideology in any army except in Russia, where the downfall of tsarism and of all the traditional ideas associated with that regime impelled a great part of the armed forces to go over to the revolutionary camp. In the other countries involved, the continuance of colonial policies and also of anti-Sovietism, maintained and enriched the panoply of ideological weapons which kept the armed forces attached to the existing social order.

The Second World War had more profound effects. The traditional armies of Eastern Europe were crushed under the weight of their defeat. A part of their members accepted the new ideological values and joined the new military structures; the rest were dispersed. But even in the victorious armies a crisis began which has not ceased to develop, in one way or another, up to the present day.

A characteristic case is that of France. Even before the Second World War there was a profound crisis in the armed forces. A section of the command never made serious preparations for defence against Germany. The gap left open by the Maginot Line, so that the invaders could encircle and capture it, was due to the 'unprofessional', political behaviour of part of the command, which had come to the conclusion that in this war, their idea of what the political and social system ought to be was no longer easy to identify with that of country, discipline, and service. . . . They faced a dilemma: which was preferable, the victory of Popular Front democracy or the triumph of fascism? The defence of their country's integrity, together with Russia, against Nazi Germany, or the defence of the traditional social order, surrendering to Germany against Russia? A part of the French high command, faced with this dilemma, renounced their country and also the maintenance and integrity of its own military instrument. Others, evidently, chose their country. The tragic and otherwise inexplicable defeat of France in 1940 was due to the political and moral crisis in her armed forces, a reflection of the crisis of the ruling classes.

It was the French people and the patriotic officers who restored the idea of country and of the national armed forces against Vichy. Later, the preponderant role of the anti-Axis imperialist powers in the liberation of France enabled the old class and colonialist order to be reconstructed, with certain modifications. The popular elements and the officers most faithful to the Resistance were practically eliminated from active service. Some of those officers who had maintained a patriotic stand rebuilt the former unity of the armed forces and rehabilitated a section of those officers who had weakened in 1940, reconstructing an army of the traditional type.

Nevertheless, this did not resolve the basic crisis, which again arose on a new terrain. The anti-fascist victory in the Second World War had irreversibly opened the era of decolonisation. Despite this, the French army was employed for long years in the military defence of a doomed colonial empire in wars such as that in Vietnam. There the professional soldiers carried the whole weight of the campaign on their shoulders; they personally experienced the wide gap between the actions they were ordered to carry out and the general attitude of the French people. They ended up by being held responsible for the loss of a war, when the real responsibility lay with the colonialist policy of the ruling classes, bankrupt and not viable in face of the Vietnamese people's resolute and indomitable will to be free.

After Vietnam came the war in Algeria. According to Charles Hernu, a part of the command, taught by the experiences in the Far East, was conscious of the inanity of this new sacrifice. But this time, use was made of conscripts, which meant that many failed to see the contradiction between military policy and the national interest until General de Gaulle himself called off the colonial adventure. In this instance the French military men employed in Algeria discovered that the very ruling class that had thrown them into this bottomless abyss was now blaming them. This created a favourable climate for the OAS (the Secret Army Organisation against Algerian independence), but at the same time deepened the crisis and gave rise to a certain revision of the role of the armed forces. The crisis did not have still greater consequences because the nuclear 'strike force' provided a new escape channel for those with a military vocation, new reasons for identifying country, service, etc., with the existing system.

This new conception of the role of the armed forces was developed within the military structures of NATO. But in the ideology emerging from these, certain traditional service concepts became blurred, and in the first place that of *country*.

NATO justifies its existence on the grounds of a possible Soviet attack. At a certain period, this still enabled country and NATO to be linked. But since for more than twenty years no Soviet aggression has taken place and the fundamentally defensive orientation of the Warsaw Pact has been confirmed, NATO is becoming a bureaucratic-military superstructure, in search of a goal with which to justify itself. In the last resort it remains above all an instrument of American political, economic and military control over Europe. This is where the idea of country gets blurred. Ultimately, nobody in any of the countries concerned knows for sure what *its* military policy or objectives are.

NATO, like any military or civil bureaucracy, generates a tendency to self-perpetuation, to grow parasitically fat. It also generates the tendency to convert itself into a power in its own right, an autonomous power over which its member states lose all real control except that which is exercised by the Pentagon and, behind it, the entire military-industrial complex of the United States and its European ramifications.

Up to now the nuclear weapon has acted as a deterrent. But it becomes ever more clear that if, as Clausewitz said, war is the continuation of politics by other means, nuclear confrontation is *not politics* because it would lead to the mutual extermination of the contestants; it rules out a victory of one over the other and the possible exploitation of such a victory, which is what can be called *politics*.

Thus, at the present time, two blocs stand face to face; they use up enormous wealth in order not to be able to use it except in mutual suicide, and sharpen the crisis of society day by day. This crisis, though it is more characteristic of the capitalist West, also affects the socialist system, not only through market relations but because the prodigious military expenditure hinders its development and absorbs a large part of its productive forces, which cannot be devoted to social progress and wellbeing.

It is certain that *tactical* nuclear weapons have arisen out of the attempt to limit the destruction and make it seem possible for war to be used in the service of politics. But any military man with experience of war knows quite well – and if he does not, then he ought to be sacked – that there is no army which manœuvred in combat order and held its positions which would not disintegrate beneath the threat of nuclear projectiles even if they were *tactical* ones. The first to run and wash their hands of the battle would be the generals.

Besides, in a continent as heavily-populated as Europe, these *tactical* weapons will indiscriminately wipe out military units, the civilian population and material wealth. There is no stable rearguard in a nuclear war, even with tactical weapons. A French Minister of the Interior, the 'Gaullist' Frey, referring during his period in office to civil defence in a possible nuclear war, said in all seriousness that he was making a list of all the existing caves in France, so as to use them for that purpose. This says every-thing, though Frey did not seem particularly aware of it: the few survivors would go back to the age of the cave-dwellers. That is to say, this situation of two mighty armed blocs, swallowing up a good part of the world's wealth, of its increasingly expensive oil and raw materials, of technological development and of the efforts of the scientists and the working people, can lead only to a return to the caves.

Charles Hernu tells of his visit to the headquarters of the Strategic Air Command in Nebraska in terrifying terms:

The rooms of the IBM operators, the offices linked directly by television with the Pentagon, the 'red telephone' never disconnected and able to alert US bases all over the world, the ships at sea, the planes in the air; the 'red clock' to mark the first minutes of the war; the guards with their pistols in open holsters, ready to gun down any officer who becomes insane . . .

The continuation of such a policy lacks all rationality, even from the standpoint of imperialist hegemony. For this reason, many political and military leaders have serious doubts about the

value of the US 'atomic umbrella', about whether or not it
would stay up if there were a conflict To these doubts should be
added another. What would Europe gain in such a desperate
situation, if the umbrella did stay up, but a larger ration of
nuclear missiles?

The consequence of this irrationality is that, according to
authoritative Italian commentators, at least as far as their
country and the sectors in which it is most interested are
concerned, it is absolutely not known what NATO's strategy is.
And it seems evident that not even in the standardisation of arms
has the organisation achieved notable results, except in the
generalised introduction of certain American weapons.
However, according to Fabrizio de Benedetti, the tanks from
this source which the Italian army has cannot be transported by
the Italian railways and have a short distance range of
independent action. All this is also reflected in a crisis of strategy
in the NATO countries. General Liuzzi writes that '. . . in Italy the
overall problem of national defence has never been – I will not
say solved – but even seriously evaluated . . .'.

Another general, Pasti, declares that 'there is no such thing as
an Italian military policy', 'no kind of serious study has been
made, on a national basis, to examine whether our armed forces
have responded to the real exigencies of Italian defence . . .',
'and we do not even know what political hypotheses should
form the starting point for the constitution of the armed
forces'.

As for France, the fluctuations of its military policy are well-
known: from colonial wars to the *force de frappe*; from all-out
defence to one-way military polarisation; from disengaging
from NATO to an ambiguous return to it. Some of the conflicts
which this situation has provoked in the high command have
also become known; it can be imagined that further down in the
chain of command the problems, perhaps less visible, are even
more profound.

The Spanish army, like Spanish society as a whole, also finds
itself in a state of transition. If it is possible to speak of an official
military policy which is reduced today to the role of auxiliary to
the United States forces and of struggle against 'internal
subversion'. Everything leads one to think that military leaders
like Lieutenant-General Diez Alegría and Lieutenant-General

Gutiérrez Mellado have broader and more modern, though not widely expressed, views on defence.

Our country's armed forces were used in the past as an instrument of colonial policy and for the defence of the bourgeois-landowners. They were subsequently given a mission of internal policy: to uphold the Franco regime. Little by little the colonies have been disappearing, under the rule of a government which proclaimed itself imperial. The last – the Sahara – did so in conditions which have left a bitter impression among the professional soldiers. Today it is proposed by authority that the armed forces uphold the monarchy and accept the changes in institutions which they previously supported.

It must be recognised that in these last thirty-six years, the army, from the professional and technical point of view, was seriously neglected. It was looked on more as an instrument of internal policy and its preparedness in all branches was neglected. Without underestimating the value of their human material, would our armed forces be in a condition to mobilise rapidly and respond effectively in the event of an attack from outside? Probably they would have to confine themselves ultimately to 'saving the honour of the flag' in a futile sacrifice. Many military men are already conscious of this, and their uneasiness is only mitigated by the thought that Spain is not really threatened, at least for the present. Some have little thought of a possible improvement of the situation, and would perhaps even regretfully give up their careers if they found other opportunities.

Others, inspired by a firm feeling of vocation for their profession, who have seen this sense of vocation turn sour, resign themselves – a state of resignation far removed from what is known in military parlance as 'being at ease'.

Our society's crisis is also shown internationally by the most able and most interested military men in many places searching for a new identity. This is evident in the interesting and important book recently published by Major Prudencio García in which he argues that armies should prepare themselves to support a policy of peace and disarmament, even though this still appears a distant prospect.

The forces of the left, and particularly we Marxists, must

actively tackle military problems as a very decisive component in
the socialist transformation of society. But we must do this by
analysing in depth the problems as they really exist today in our
societies, and not as they presented themselves in the years of the
First World War or even earlier. Hence, though the Marxist
method of analysis continues to be the only one capable of
leading us to correct conclusions, it is most erroneous to repeat
today formulas used by Marxists in the past, which leads to
Marxism being turned into a mere mouthing of dogmatic
phrases.

Society cannot be transformed without transforming the
State and consequently transforming one of its basic
instruments, the army. But in opting for a democratic road as we
have done, not for the sake of convenience, nor because we are
in some sort of beatific state, but because of inescapable
historical imperatives, we must ask ourselves whether it is
possible to establish a convergence between the general
orientation of the forces striving for socialism and this search for
a new identity now prevalent among the most realistic military
men.

It is not a matter here of politicising the army in a direction
different from that which it has followed, and even less of
military plots, of repeating today the history of the nineteenth
and part of the twentieth century in our country, with its
pronunciamientos, its coups d'état and civil wars, but of attaining
an identification between the army and civilian society in this
epoch of transition, an identification which supersedes the
historic equation: *oligarchy + armed forces = conservatism and
reaction*, and which assists the democratic advance of the
progressive forces towards a just and equal society.

The armed revolutions destroyed the old type of army root
and branch in order to create a new one. This happened in the
socialist revolutions and also in the great French Revolution,
which was bourgeois in character. In the specific conditions of
the developed countries of the capitalist West this prospect, save
for unforeseeable cataclysms, does not seem possible. In
envisaging today the transformation of society and the State in
these countries, the problem of the armed forces must be
approached differently. But it must be tackled; it cannot be
avoided.

A serious analysis cannot ignore the fact that even in those cases in which the apparatus of the oppressor State was destroyed by force, such a result was gained when the revolutionary forces succeeded in winning over or neutralising the decisive part of the military apparatus, as a result of that apparatus's defeat and the subsequent crisis of established society and its military structures.

The question is *whether a democratic transformation of the military mentality can be attained as a result of a social crisis, due to factors other than war*. If the reply were negative, one would have to renounce socialism and be eternally resigned to the social and political *status quo*, or else hope for the outbreak of war, which would be insane (we have already seen that with modern weapons this would mean the mutual suicide of all contending classes).

Definitely, the forces of change in the developed capitalist countries can only try to win over or neutralise the greater part if not the whole of the army by other than traditional means. This requires a drastic revision of the attitude of the forces of change towards the military apparatus, a new approach to the whole question, capable of accepting certain characteristics of the military mentality and of extending and deepening within it the objective effects of the present crisis in society.

It is clear that the old anti-militarist attitudes, pure political agitation, a negative approach to the army, would not facilitate the task but would make it impossible and would help the ruling oligarchy to form a bloc with the army.

For the new strategy, one must start from an objective fact: as long as the State exists, whatever its social content, the army, with one structure or another, is an indispensable instrument. No state, capitalist or socialist, has renounced the army. In a general way, armies will disappear when states wither away, when society has attained a communist structure on a world scale. This is our ultimate aim, but it must be realistically recognised that this is still a long way off. In other words, we regard the existence of the army as a social necessity. But the army, and this is a fundamental principle, must above all be the instrument which safeguards national independence and sovereignty, and not the organ which secures the oppression of the monopolist oligarchy over the other classes and social strata, or the inviolability of the capitalist political and social *status quo*.

The army should not in any way be a police reserve. The army, its commanding officers, should be accessible to the popular sectors. It should not be the instrument of a party or faction of society. Within the framework of its specific functions – the defence of territorial integrity – it must obey the orders of whatever government is established as a result of universal suffrage. If any government, and still more so any faction in society, should try to use it for functions other than its own, it should firmly refuse to obey.

Of all the ideas with which the army has been imbued, there is one that must be banished: that of *blind* discipline towards all authority emanating from the constituted social order, *blind* discipline towards the orders of the higher command. Discipline is indispensable in an army, and without it there would be no army; but discipline, even in the army, cannot be *blind and unconditional*. The soldier is a man, not a robot. Nothing excuses a soldier, whatever his rank, if he carries out an order which goes against the sovereign will of the people or against human dignity.

In this respect, the world war against fascism resulted in the establishment of what could be called a kind of jurisprudence based on well-defined ethical principles. Members of the armed forces who committed war crimes were not covered by the orders of their superiors; they were judged and sentenced for not having disobeyed them. In other words, it was their *blind and unconditional* obedience to the higher command that was punished.

During the Vietnam war, serious elements of decomposition developed in the ranks of the US army, and these war crimes, and the revulsion which a section of the officers and men felt towards them, were one of the factors leading to the US retreat and withdrawal. The more notorious of these crimes were even the subject of trials in the United Sates, which, though they did not lead to the severe punishment of those responsible – because they were too senior – did contribute towards finally discrediting the unjust war.

I do not, as I write, have the text of the French military regulation revised after the war in Algeria and must rely on memory. But I remember that I was favourably impressed by its clauses. These gave junior officers a margin of judgement and freedom not to carry out a certain type of order which would result in an attack on human dignity and the spirit of democratic legality.

Apart from this notion of blind discipline towards orders from above, others which go to make up the military mentality – patriotism, the spirit of service and sacrifice – are perfectly valid and noble, and are absolutely necessary in any type of army.

The army and society as it exists must be brought together. This, in the first place, poses the question of the social position of the officers and senior military commanders. That is to say, concretely, on what should the *social prestige* of the corps of officers and the high command be based?

There is a concept of *social prestige*, for example, which had its origin in the colonial wars. According to this concept, the military leadership in general derived its *social prestige* from its mission, which was to intervene in wars of that type, to be ready to sacrifice their lives in them, for what they had been taught to regard as the 'interests of the country' even though these were only the interests of a ruling class wanting to exploit the colonies economically. This mission, which involved for the commanders the risk of their lives, gave them *social prestige*, conferred on them a title of superiority over the rest of the citizens. The military command was officially the *saviour of the fatherland*, which slipped easily from '*saving*' it in the colonised country to *saving* it against their own country, when the ruling class considered itself to be threatened by the oppressed classes.

In order to *interest* the army directly in its own ends, the ruling class drew a part of the higher officers, the top of the pyramid of military discipline, into the management boards of enterprises, into direct participation in business; although among the general run of officers the inculcation of this conception of class took place through a blindly stratified discipline and an *ad hoc* ideological conditioning. The economic position of the vast majority of these officers was that of the lower-middle strata of society.

Can this idea of the social prestige of the military continue, now that there are no colonies and that the army has no reason to take on the role of saviour, unless it is solely from its own people?

Today, the military cadre should occupy in the country the role of a technician, a scientist, an intellectual educator of men skilled in protecting our territory from outside attack. In the event of war, the professional military man is not the only *saviour of the nation,* since in such circumstances an infinite number of civilian professionals also become military personnel who defend their country's integrity just as he does and as do the NCOs and soldiers under their command. Moreover, this category of technician or scientist, that is to say, of intellectual, is determined not only by the officer's function as an educator of men but also by the complexity, the growing sophistication of military technology.

Today the command of a modern military unit has nothing in common with the command of the troops of the old Foreign Legion or of the traditional colonial infantry. Physical courage and a forceful character are not enough to make a good commander, even though they are indispensable; broad knowledge is needed, a real intellectual training. The officer who aspires to a full military career must in practice be a technician, an engineer, a scientist. He should possess a university education in the broadest sense; and this not only in the technical field, but also in the humanist and sociological subjects. For increasingly, in a society which is developing scientifically and technically, in which people are more enlightened and have a higher estimation of their own worth and personal dignity, the forms in which command is exercised also vary. The officer no longer receives into the barracks men who are mostly illiterate, timorous, meek, ready to obey any order as long as it is given sternly and even with brutality. He receives educated men – sometimes better educated than himself – who reason, think, and look at him critically. If he is not intellectually prepared to command men of this type, the loyalty they give him will be purely formal; he will have no real command over them and true discipline will not exist; in time of battle – which is what, after all, the army prepares for – this could have totally negative consequences, which would be negative in any circumstances. In modern society, an officer, before he can be an efficient commander, must more and more be able to convince his men that he *knows how to command* and inspire their confidence, not, I repeat, by treating them with brutality, but by his qualifications and intelligence.

Hence a democratic military policy must, to begin with, set out to reform the system of officers' training, which would have to take the forms of a mixed system of training in both the specifically military academies and in the university.

The military academies should devote themselves to the teaching of the doctrines, strategy, tactics and the specifically military applications of technology; but the cadet should attend the university for courses in science and technology, the humanities and sociology, together with the rest of the students. Those officers and commanders who are already trained should be able to take university courses to complete and develop their qualifications.

In other words, the officers of a modern army ought to be a highly-educated group, whose *social prestige* is based on their intellectual qualifications and not on the fact that they bear arms and wear a uniform which distinguishes them from others. In fact, already in modern armies a trained officer can, in civilian life, be a technician, an engineer, an economist, a sociologist, in conditions similar to those of any graduate. This tendency is becoming constantly more pronounced.

The combination of training in the academy and in the university will enable the officer to have not only a more complete education, but contact and direct knowledge, before entering the barracks, with young people who are going to enter the army and who, if they ever have to defend the country, are going to shed their blood at his side.

This training should also enable military personnel, if they want to and it is necessary for them to do so, to go over to civilian life at a reasonable level, without a reduction of status. This is important because not everyone who takes up the profession of officer can reach the rank of general.

Nevertheless, in a modern war even generals, when they command operational units, have got to be young. That is to say, they have to be in top physical condition to take full command of troops and the management of extremely complicated military apparatus, which demands an alert intellect and an agile physique. If this is true of the generals who command big units, it is even more so of the colonels, lieutenant-colonels, majors, etc., who head smaller units and who in a war today may either bring a battle to a successful conclusion or be wiped out in minutes.

This means that the operational units of a modern army must be under the command of young officers and leaders. This would logically entail a lowering of the retirement age for some. Because of this, a military man would leave active service – except possibly the most gifted who might have a position on the general staff or in the military academies – when in possession of all his intellectual faculties and when reducing him to inactivity would be tantamount to premature death. It is precisely a broader education that would enable such a person to enter civilian life at a certain age and continue to do a job in keeping with his skills and without loss of status.

This would also accord with the modern conception that the defence of one's country is not the exclusive function of the professional soldier; that defence is not the privileged sacrifice of a minority of saviours but the job of all citizens, of the whole people. The task of the professional is, in fact, to fight, if there is a war. But in that case, officers, NCOs and soldiers of the reserve – non-professionals – will fight just as he does. What distinguishes the professional soldier from them is that, in peacetime, his job involves giving military training to these non-professionals, which to some extent can be compared to the work of university teachers in the civilian disciplines, except that the social scope of their work is infinitely broader.

That is to say, *in this modern conception, the military man is not a member of a kind of closed order, isolated from and above society but a participant in a teaching body devoted to imparting certain specific information to the citizens so that they can defend the country's territorial integrity in case of need.*

This concept is certainly not that of the present capitalist State. But even within this State, above all if we succeed in turning its ideological apparatuses against it, this conception can progressively win over very broad sections of military men, because it is, in addition, based on objective factors, and on a historical tendency which is · daily becoming more sharply defined.

These factors, this tendency, are connected on the one hand with the development of the productive forces which are generally first applied to the technique and art of war, and which, because of their growing sophistication, demand ever higher qualifications from the professional soldier; on the other hand, with the role of the armies, which are an instrument of State policy and, in a world which is not yet homogeneous, in which different social regimes coexist, in which colonial empires have disappeared and in which there is developing – though slowly and painfully – a process of democratisation of international relations and of internationalisation in all respects, this State policy is being transformed profoundly and sometimes imperceptibly.

For this reason there is in the developed capitalist States what we might call a crisis of military doctrine, this being understood in a wider sense than that of ordinary rules and regulations. The definition of the army's mission is in a constant state of revision. Hence the deep crisis in NATO. The changing of the world balance of forces, which in the past took place almost regularly through war between the various States, has now become taboo, because of its prohibitive practical consequences, a result of the so-called *nuclear deterrent*.

Today there is an equilibrium which came into being after the Second World War and the upheavals it caused. It is a balance which rests on the military hegemony of the two great powers, the USA and the USSR. Unless there is a moment of insanity which would destroy the planet, this equilibrium cannot be changed in a direct confrontation. Hence the undeniable advances of coexistence, however precarious – and they are precarious because they rest on nuclear weapons and not on the need for a new international order, now gradually gaining universal recognition.

Though the present equilibrium is not static and is, little by little, changing, this change does not keep within the traditions. For this reason, military doctrines based on the idea of confrontation between two blocs, an idea which every day seems more ominous and irrational for both sides, are in crisis. The possibility of such confrontation ceases to be a *policy*, for a policy always pursues an objective with at least a minimal possibility of realisation, with at least a minimum of rationality.

The change in the present balance points to a lessening of bi-polarisation and the creation of a new multi-polar balance. In Asia and in Europe, new poles of power are springing up. The so-called Third World, with its unequal levels and its contradictions, is tending to become a new pole, though its military power is far behind its potential influence in the economic and political fields.

World problems and contradictions appear today, above all, in the political and economic spheres. Except in backward countries whose military resources, even with external aid, go no further than the traditional weapons, it is very difficult to imagine a military confrontation. Without doubt the general staffs have plans for such possible confrontations; but between the blueprint and the actuality there is a great gulf. What army today could stand up to a battle, even if fought with simple tactical nuclear weapons, without melting into thin air in physical and moral disintegration? What unit would be able to remain in combat formation in the field facing such weapons? What rearguard could resist without crumbling?

At a recent meeting of the leaders of the Second International the doubt was already expressed – a doubt long held by politicians such as De Gaulle and others, though some did not admit it – as to whether the American nuclear umbrella would function in the event of a conflict in Europe. In the same way, there was no Soviet atomic umbrella either in Vietnam, Cuba or the Middle East.

From this well-founded doubt comes the idea of European defence, and new conceptions of regional defence may arise, which are perhaps inevitable stages on the road towards a new world order based on general disarmament, if the necessity and urgency of that does not impose itself sooner as something entirely obvious.

In any case the policy – and with it the resulting military doctrine – of bi-polarisation is in a state of crisis. It is so, moreover, because every policy of blocs, whatever the ideology on which it rests, presupposes hegemony; hegemony of the strongest power in the political, economic and military fields. This is an objective fact which no ideology can conceal. And this hegemony, which begins by drawing its sustenance from military power and adopting the attitude of a protector, ends by extending itself to all aspects: political, economic, moral, cultural. In one way or another that hegemony ends up by becoming intolerable in the eyes of those who suffer it.

Contradictions emerge in each bloc and these become sharper precisely when the object of this policy – the possible military confrontation with the opposing bloc – appears in an increasingly obvious way as a nonsense, as suicide.

Confining oneself to the problems of military doctrine in this phase of transition on a world scale, for countries like ours, which cannot aspire to becoming powers like the 'great' ones, the first objective, strictly from the viewpoint of national defence and the renunciation of an aggressive war, must be to make sure that the aggressor realises the prohibitive cost of an invasion, disproportionate to any results, arising from the fact that – according to deeply rooted national traditions, in the case of Spain – every citizen would take up arms and defend every inch of ground, and even in the event of occupation would not capitulate and would make life impossible for the invaders. Such a policy could also involve cooperation with neighbouring countries in similar circumstances.

But a war of national defence, in those conditions, would have to be a *war of the whole people*. It could not be a war in the interests of an oligarchic class or on behalf of interests foreign to the country's. Military cooperation with other countries would have to be based on the fact that they were being threatened or attacked by the same aggressor.

Indispensable in such a case is an army at one with the nation, with the people; it should be the people itself in arms. This means that alongside the standing army, founded on recruitment, there should be a reserve army, made up of fit men on a regional basis, training at regular intervals and in a position to take up arms and wage defensive battles in their region, or to intervene in other places in a matter of hours. This concept of the national, popular war of defence is in total opposition to the imperialist conception of conquest and, of course, to the idea of an anti-subversive war waged against one's own people. At bottom the idea of an anti-subversive war corresponds to a counter-revolutionary army, trained not to defend the nation but to prepare a coup d'état, not to preserve territorial integrity but to protect the privileges of an oligarchic minority.

The forces of society standing for change have to wage an open struggle for the type of army capable of assuming national

defence, of setting the national interest against that of the ruling
oligarchies. In this sphere it is possible to win the understanding
and sympathy of the professional soldiers who are dedicated to
their job.

The army must start by having its main sources of supply
within the country; it must not depend on foreign countries, not
at least for essentials, for its arms and ammunition. Which
means that a national arms industry is required, suited to the
country's possibilities; and that national industrial development is also necessary which, in the event of war, could assure
the means of defence. It follows that *the socialist forces and, in
the first place, the Communist Party, must have a military policy.* Only
by possessing a more rational, more national, more attractive
military policy then that of the monopolist oligarchic State, can
they, before and after reaching government, win the
professional military men for that policy and make certain that
the majority of them will loyally support the new State power.

This means winning over a section of society, deformed
ideologically, which can be attracted through professional
motives and by a different ideology which does not suppress
psychological reactions but adapts them to the new realities of
Spanish society and the world.

The struggle to win over this section makes it necessary to deal
seriously with its problems, get to know them, and to endeavour
to provide a solution for them which is in the national interest. A
political programme of the socialist forces must embody
solutions to the problems of national defence and the armed
forces.

Some Spanish 'traditionalists' would say that this is a plan for
'subversion'. Why subversion? It could perhaps be the start of a
plan for the democratisation of the army and of the concept of
defence, which, starting from the national interest, will operate
in favour of the army itself and of the position of the military
man in society; of a plan to defend and develop publicly, for the
problem of defence and the armed forces is of such importance
that it justifies the broadest permanent debate in society. In this
sense it is not a question of bringing politics into the army, but
of bringing the military theme into the realm of left-wing
politics, in such a way that it is not only the right, which
traditionally controls the State, that gives political inspiration to

the army, so that the army ceases to be identified with the right and becomes ever more closely identified with the nation by which it is nurtured and whose defence it should be.

The elaboration of a democratic policy on both the police and the army, which – though still made in opposition – is already contributing towards providing a certain basis of support.for the socialist forces of change within both these coercive apparatuses, and the formulation of a series of measures to be applied by government along the same lines, are issues of the greatest importance for us. To them can be added the question of the democratic reform of public office and, in general, the thorough democratisation of the administration.

In this last respect, the bringing of the State apparatus closer to the country, to the people, is especially urgent. This would include the decentralisation of that vast machine, the setting up of regional organs of power, and, in Spain – which contains various nationalities side by side – of national organs of power. The Napoleonic centralist tradition was that of an imperialist State which, directed toward external conquest, concentrated the energies of the country into a single unit. A democratic state should be marked by decentralisation, so that the administration functions more flexibly, closer to and more in agreement with the will of the governed. A State of this kind could be transformed more easily into one ready to arrive at socialism by a democratic road, into a State more easily controlled by the people's elected representatives and, as a result, would be better protected against the dangers of an armed coup.

This decentralisation is, moreover, a necessity for the economic development of the regions and the nationalities, for the overcoming of the imbalances which make some zones into veritable economic urban monstrosities and keep others in a state of backwardness and underdevelopment.

It is a question of creating a living democracy at all levels throughout the country – a democracy in which effective power will reside in the organs of popular power so that the vitality of that power is such that no group installed in the central zone of power could wipe it out at a blow.

This conception of the State and of the struggle to democratise it presupposes the renunciation of the idea, in its traditional form, of *a workers' and peasants' State*; of a State, that is, built from scratch, bringing into its offices workers from the factories and peasants from the land and sending the functionaries who had hitherto worked in the offices to occupy their places. Such a State has never really existed, except as an ideal. Even where the revolution triumphed by an act of force, the bureaucracy, with some exceptions, has continued as such and the new functionaries have rapidly acquired many of the bad habits of the old.

This conception of the State also means giving up the ideas of a State apparatus that is a party apparatus, a State apparatus controlled by a party apparatus; it is a question of creating a State apparatus which at every moment faithfully obeys the people's elected representatives and which cannot be manipulated against the will of the people.

It may be that the transformation of the present State of monopoly capital into a State fit for the exercise of the hegemony of the anti-monopolist socialist forces and, specifically, of the new historic bloc, the alliance of the forces of labour and culture – it may be that this cannot be won solely through political action and democratic government measures; it can happen that at a given moment it may be necessary to reduce by *force* resistance by *force*; that is to say that the qualitative transformation of this apparatus may not be entirely peaceful and a democratic government may find itself confronted with an attempted coup. But if it has the support of the people, democratically won in fair fight, and if it has carried out an intelligent policy of democratising the State apparatus, both in opposition and in government, it will find itself in a favourable position to complete its work and sweep away the remnants of the oligarchic hegemony.

4

The Model of Democratic Socialism

It is certainly the case that the democratic road to socialism presupposes a process of economic transformations different from what we might regard as the *classical* model. That is to say that it presupposes *the long-term coexistence of public and private forms of property*. It is in this way that the stage of political and economic democracy foreseen in our programme acquires its full significance; in this stage, which is not yet socialism, but which is also no longer the domination of the State by monopoly capital, it is a question of preserving to the greatest possible extent the productive forces and social services already created, recognising the role which private enterprise has in this phase.

At the same time, the main aim is to socialise – and in certain cases not only at State level but at that of the national, regional and local authorities – the decisive levers of the economy so as to ensure the hegemony of the historic bloc made up of the forces of labour and culture in the transition period.

At the same time, the fact that those levers are socialised should be the basis for democratic planning, on a national scale, of the economy, which will integrate the public and private sectors and make it possible to work out an economic model adapted to the real needs of the population and to radical improvement in the quality of living.

I am speaking of rational planning based on the requirements of that new economic model and quality of life, and of democratic planning in the sense that it should begin to be

worked out from below, incorporating the initiative, needs and
possibilities of each section of the population and of each
enterprise or service, and also the fact that the general plan
should take shape as the coordination, in a single whole, of
many plans, at all levels, and not as something bureaucratically
imposed from above.

In that planning, and in our country's conditions, primary
attention must be paid to crop farming and livestock breeding
so as to solve in an effective way – depending as little as possible
on imports – the problem of *foodstuffs* and, at the same time, to
deal with the acute social and economic injustices suffered by
that sector which has traditionally been shamefully neglected.
Spain can produce meat, cereals, vegetables, fruit, oil-bearing
crops, sugar and wine in sufficient quantities to meet her own
needs and to export. This should be an economic aim of prime
importance. Closely linked with this is the need to organise the
industrial transformation of crop and livestock production in
which the agricultural producers must have a direct interest, as
well as to reorganise the distributive networks. This will also
help to prevent the movement of capital from the countryside.

In the agrarian sector it will be necessary to combine the
preservation of private enterprise with various degrees and
forms of cooperativism related to production, processing and
distribution, forms which should be encouraged as much from
the point of view of economic yield as from that of social
transformation. In this connection it should be explained that
the slogan: 'The land for those who cultivate it!' does not
necessarily mean the individual parcelling out of land; it can
also be realised with collective forms or with mixed forms,
individual and cooperative, so that social justice and economic
yield are in harmony.

In order to solve the problem of foodstuffs, considerable help
and a great deal of attention must likewise be given to the fishing
industry. The problems which arise from the extension of the
limits of coastal waters by the Common Market and other
countries must be tackled not only in the context of foreign
policy – although this is necessary – but also through the
transformation and modernisation of the fishing fleet so that
our fishing can be undertaken with the most advanced technical
means. The State should make a decisive contribution towards

this, as should also the national, regional and local authorities; in addition cooperative forms of ownership should be encouraged.

Democratic planning should be centred likewise on the *development of sources of energy*, with the policy of making our country as independent as possible of supplies from abroad. The State should pay much greater attention to the search for oil deposits, to the development and modernisation of the mining industry, and to scientific research aimed at profiting from all the natural sources of energy.

The problems of *foodstuffs* and *energy* are today vital for any modern State; and both are fundamental to ensure balanced development and general well-being.

Rational and democratic planning should concentrate on improving the quality of life in the big towns, ending land speculation, solving the housing problem in a satisfactory way, developing the various communal social services, and organising transport so that passengers are less inconvenienced and pollution is reduced. It is likewise essential to improve the living conditions in the rural townships, bringing them the benefits of civilisation and culture, while tending to overcome the differences between town and country.

Education must be another of the essential aspects of rational democratic planning. The role of education, in all spheres, no matter where, has been amply demonstrated; education is not only necessary for the upbringing of the new man; it is also a productive force which intervenes decisively in economic development. Free education for children and young people, and also for adult students, is essential to promote the intellectual advance of the working people and their children. However, contrary to a seemingly very radical point of view, it should also be enjoyed by the children of the well-to-do, since this will help to encourage their material and ideological independence from the family environment, to emphasise the role of society as a collective and, objectively, to overcome the conception of education and of the family itself as an ideological apparatus for 'reproducing the production relations' of capitalism.

The health service and medicine are another of the great social tasks; out-patient departments, clinics, hospitals,

preventive medicine, research – all these must be of vital
concern to society. The socialisation of medicine remains a great
goal to be achieved; it cannot, however, be satisfactorily arrived
at by administrative and coercive measures in face of the free
exercise of the profession, but with the multiplication of
resources adequate for medical and health service care and for
research, and with the training of plenty of well-qualified
personnel, properly paid and with a proper social status.

Without in any way presuming to enter into an exhaustive
definition of the aims of planning, or to draw up any complete
plan, it is obviously necessary to include technological
modernisation, the development of our better-off key
industries, and help for our traditional industries like, for
example, the textile, footwear and other industries.

The coexistence of forms of public and private ownership
means acceptance of unearned increment and the private
appropriation of part of this, i.e. the existence of a mixed
system. Society has the means to ensure that this unearned
increment is not exorbitant, by means of taxation, and that it
is nevertheless sufficient to encourage private enterprise.
Moreover, by controlling credit, it has the opportunity to
channel savings towards the purposes best suited to the country
as a whole. This system, which will still be economically mixed,
will translate itself into a political regime in which the owners
will be able to organise themselves not only economically but
also in a political party or parties representative of their
interests; this will be one of the component parts of political and
ideological pluralism. All this also means that the class struggle
is going to manifest itself openly, although the social consensus
will logically be greater than that which exists in present-day
society in which hegemony is exercised by monopoly capital.
The overcoming of social differences will follow a natural
process and will not be the result of coercive measures but of the
development of the productive forces and of the social services,
so that through a gradual process, encouraged by education, all
sections of the population will be integrating themselves in the
social collective.

In other words, under social and political democracy there
will still be social differences which will not be disguised, but
open. But the dominant position of the public sector in the

economy and the political hegemony of the forces of labour and culture will ensure a progressive advance towards a classless, equitable society, towards socialism.

This road opens up the possibility of incorporating in the new society, not only the mass of scientists and technicians, but also that new figure in modern industry to whom the term 'executive' has been applied, always providing that he values his function in a professional capacity more than his share, if any, in the ownership of the enterprise. Under social and political democracy, and in a socialist society as well, the functions performed by the executive – naturally, with certain differences – will also be needed. Many socialist countries have had to improvise their executives, sometimes at too high an economic and social cost. This is a danger to be avoided as far as possible. Certainly in the new social forms, the executive will have to take the democracy of the shop floor into account and will function within an overall plan. But these restrictions will certainly be no greater and, indeed, will be more justified from the social standpoint than those imposed upon him today by the planning of the enterprise and management decisions. Moreover, he will experience the inner satisfaction of the social value of his work being recognised, not just by a monopoly group, but by the whole of the collective.

SOVIET THINKING AND THE DEMOCRATIC ROAD

I can already hear doctrinaire people crying out that this is 'sheer reformism'. That does not frighten me. Let us take a look at the socialist countries which have carried out their revolution along a classical road. The greater part of them have already experienced whole decades with the new regime, and while the taking of power was carried out at an extremely rapid tempo from the historical point of view, the economic and social transformation is proceeding at a much slower pace. Examples of inequality still continue. There are vital problems, such as the standard of living and the supplying of the population with goods and foodstuffs, which cannot be considered solved. Problems of productivity, of participation, are on the agenda. And there remains the great unsolved question – that of democracy, and social contradictions which a one-sided propaganda hides but does not solve. To mention all this is not to deny the great progress made in those countries in comparison with the past.

The Chinese comrades repeat, without beating about the bush, that in their country the class struggle continues and is reflected in the internal struggle in the ruling party itself. Arguments of this kind were taken to the extreme limit in the USSR by Stalin in order to establish his personal power in the party and in the State. In these arguments there is an element of manipulation to suit the convenience of established power. But there is also an element of reality. This is that even in those˙ countries where power was taken overnight the process of social transformation is necessarily slow. Lenin said that for the Russian proletariat it had been easier to take power than it was for the proletariat in the West, but that it would be more difficult for the Russian proletariat to carry out the social transformation (I do not have the actual quotation to hand, but this is the general sense of it). It is very probable, given the economic and cultural development of the West, that although the process of the changeover of power may be slower along this road which we are advocating, the results of the social changes may come much more rapidly and more tangibly for the working people.

To put it very briefly, the question which confronts the Marxist revolutionaries of the seventies is this: Shall we tackle our tasks in order to develop the socialist revolution, making it *worldwide*, with a scientific criterion, on the basis of *a concrete analysis of concrete reality*, or shall we tackle them with ideological oversimplification, with an intellectual laziness comparable with that of those people who repeat elsewhere: 'God made the world in six days and he rested on the seventh day'?

What is the concrete reality of the present day? This reality is that in spite of the strength which it still has, imperialism, as a social system, has been disestablished, first of all by the Great October Socialist Revolution, then by the advance of socialism, with its limitations, shortcomings and imperfections – which we do not hide and have no interest in hiding – in Europe, Asia, Latin America, and through the whole process of decolonisation. This process of disestablishment is going deeper every day and is driving forward currents making for transformations in the countries which up to now have dominated the world.

We are in the midst of a worldwide revolutionary process. This process started from violent revolutions, above all from the most classic of them – the Russian Revolution – which, historically speaking, has had in relation to the future world socialist system a place equivalent to that occupied by the great French Revolution in relation to the bourgeois system.

That process is having repercussions in, and is reaching, all corners of the earth, in various forms, even though its epicentre was the October Revolution. The bourgeois revolution had its epicentre in France; in no other country at that time did an uprising take place which transformed the social order so radically. But the ideas of the French Revolution spread over the whole of the west of Europe and, through unsuccessful revolutionary movements, wars and structural reforms, determined to a large extent by the progress of the productive forces, the bourgeois system spread over the whole of Europe, with different processes in each country.

Why then should we not conceive of the extension of socialism on a world scale as a multiform process which had its starting point in the October Revolution, continued with the anti-fascist victory, and with the social changes in the East (the revolutions in China, Vietnam, Cambodia, Laos), in Cuba, and in certain Arab and African countries – with their own specific features – as a result of which the historically dominant imperialist countries lost their hegemonic role; a process in which the new correlation of forces developing within these countries brings about advances, without mathematically repeating the historical models, through overall structural changes which, at a certain level of accumulation, give rise to a qualitative leap, from the bourgeois to the socialist order, on the basis of each country's indigenous political conditions? The revolutionary movements which have developed in the last half century and more in these countries, the armed resistance to fascism, the mighty class struggles to which they are witness, will have been the national antecedents of these structural changes and will have driven them forward, opening the way to socialist democratic processes.

As with the bourgeois transformation in many cases, this road will mean that a part of the ruling classes in the kind of society that is dying will – under the global weight of socialism, and of the new problems caused by the confrontation between the ex-colonisers and the ex-colonised, and of economic developments like the explosive pressure of the capitalist and imperialist systems due to the increase in the productive forces and the worldwide struggle for equal relations between nations – become more susceptible to 'influence and will be able to cooperate in various ways with the new social system, so that the scope and possibilities of violent resistance may be reduced to minority groups from these classes.

We often say that the developed capitalist world is ripe for socialism. Let us draw the conclusions which follow from this statement. Through phenomena which are still sometimes surrounded by immense confusion, it can be seen that the people are becoming aware of this reality perhaps more quickly than we think, although sometimes this is not so clear to us, because it is probably happening in a different, less simplified form than we have all our lives imagined.

There is no doubt that this process is not going to happen automatically, without the revolutionary will of the forces of progress and action ensuing from this, which may sometimes go through phases of violence, imposed by the ruling classes; but the revolutionary will should put at the disposal of its strategy an analysis of the real possibilities and consider clearly what is new in the situation so as not to become ineffective through blind mimicry.

When Khrushchev and the Soviet leadership, at the Twentieth Congress of the Communist Party of the Soviet Union, roughly sketched out the policy of 'Destalinisation', some of these problems were already beginning to present themselves, in a more or less confused way, to the Soviet communists.

In his report at that Congress, Khrushchev recalled what Lenin had said on the eve of the October Revolution:

All nations will arive at socialism – this is inevitable, but not all will do so in exactly the same way, each will contribute something of its own in one or another form of democracy, one or another variety of the dictatorship of the proletariat, one or another rate at which socialist transformations will be effected in the various aspects of social life. There is nothing more primitive from the point of view of theory or more ridiculous from that of practice than to paint, 'in the name of historical materialism', this aspect of the future in a monotonous grey.

The result will be nothing more than crude daubing (*Report of the Central Committee to the 20th Congress of the Communist Party*, London, 1956, p. 29).

And Khrushchev added on his own account:

It is probable that more forms of transition to socialism will appear. Moreover, the implementation of these forms need not be associated with civil war under all circumstances. . . . It is not true that we regard violence and civil war as the only way to remake society.

In this connection [Khrushchev's report continues] the question arises of whether it is possible to go over to socialism by using parliamentary means. . . . At the same time the present situation offers the working class in a number of capitalist countries a real opportunity to unite the overwhelming majority of the people under its leadership and to secure the transfer of the basic means of production into the hands of the people. The right-wing parties and their bourgeois governments are suffering bankruptcy with increasing frequency. In these circumstances the working class, by rallying around itself the working peasantry, the intelligentsia, all patriotic forces and resolutely repulsing the opportunist elements who are incapable of giving up the policy of compromise with the capitalists and landlords, is in a position to defeat the reactionary forces opposed to the interests of the people, to capture a stable majority in parliament, and transfer the latter from an organ of bourgeois democracy into a genuine instrument of the people's will . . .

The winning of a stable parliamentary majority backed by a mass revolutionary movement of the proletariat and of all the working people could create for the working class of a number of capitalist . . . countries the conditions needed to secure fundamental social changes (ibid., p. 30).

If I bring up the way in which Khrushchev presented the question at the Twentieth Congress, this is not in order to produce an *authoritative argument*. I do not have much faith in authoritative arguments, and Khrushchev's was contradicted quite a while ago by his own party colleagues, who refer less and less frequently to the Twentieth Congress. Moreover, the way Khrushchev's report was expressed, if one judges by what has happened since, would seem to have been in response to an intuition, arising perhaps from the need to make a breakthrough towards the West and overcome the Cold War, rather than as a profound analysis of concrete reality and the diversity of problems which this brought in its train. It was, however, a rough draft in which a new reality made itself felt, still carrying forward ideological elements and formulas from the previous reality.

But knowing, as we do, the way in which reports of this kind are drawn up – a process in which recourse is had to the collaboration of the accredited theoreticians, who work on them for months, elaborating formulas and then remodelling them – in other words, knowing that they are not just a product of individual improvisation, it is reasonable to conclude that at that time those theoreticians had revised and corrected certain theses of Lenin about the *limitations of universal suffrage* and of the democracy practised under bourgeois regimes – classical theses to which scholastic doctrinaires continue to be firmly tied. And fundamentally this revision did more or less take account of the concrete reality of that period; it was done, therefore, in a Marxist spirit, even though it may still have been incomplete and contradictory, the fruit of thinking that had not been finalised and was still caught in the grip of dogma.

A MORE FUNDAMENTAL ASSESSMENT OF DEMOCRACY

In the course of political and theoretical polemics and in the midst of the class struggle, and above all when this struggle becomes tense and sharp, the way in which all questions are posed, including those arising on a scientific basis and concerned with principles, has a degree of subjectivity which is determined not only by deep feeling but also by the rigorous necessity to outline immediate political tasks, without leaving any excuse for vacillation. Emphasis is placed on what is on the agenda for immediate action, and this also involves a descent into propagandist exaggeration, because doubt about the need for this or that initiative can strengthen the enemy and jeopardise the success of the entire strategy. Sometimes, however, later on, as the strategy develops, that exaggeration has to be discreetly rectified. I recall, for instance, Lenin's subsequent explanation, in what was already a different situation, of the exaggerated way in which, during the polemics with the Mensheviks about the structure of the workers' party – in works such as *What is to be Done?* – emphasis had been put on the idea of a party of 'professional revolutionaries'. Or else – another example –

when Engels explains that if the disciples of Marxism sometimes lay more stress than they should on the economic side, with reference to historical materialism, the blame rests with Marx and himself, because in face of adversaries who denied it, they had to emphasise this main principle, at the expense of other elements involved in the interaction. This points to the difference between the position of the researcher, pure and simple, who is not involved in action and who is working in laboratory conditions, and that of the Marxist revolutionary, who is also engaged in research, but in the midst of *practice* in which the will also has an important role and is the factor which gives to politics the significance, not only of a science, but also of an art.

In this connection we cannot overlook the enlightening letter from Engels to Joseph Bloch:

. . . history is made in such a way that the final result always arises from conflicts between many individual wills, of which each again has been made what it is by a host of particular conditions of life. Thus there are innumerable intersecting forces, an infinite series of parallelograms of forces which give rise to one resultant – the historical event. This may again itself be viewed as the product of a power which works as a whole, *unconsciously* and without volition. For what each individual wills is obstructed by everyone else, and what emerges is something which no one willed. . . . But from the fact that individual wills . . . do not obtain what they want, but are merged into an aggregate mean, a common resultant, it must not be concluded that they are equal to zero. On the contrary, each contributes to the resultant and is to this extent included in it (Marx/Engels, *Selected Works*, London, 1968, p. 683).

The tendency to emphasise what is of paramount importance at the given moment, even with the danger of exaggerating it, to the extent of making one-sided and excessive generalisations, is, I believe, apparent in some of Lenin's wiring, on the eve of the October Revolution and in the midst of the Revolution, when the defence of the young Soviet power was literally a question of life or death. Far be it from me to reproach the great revolutionary leader for what is common – in his case with genius, and without it in others – to all revolutionaries.

In his polemics against the reformist tendencies which lauded 'democracy' as against the prospect or the reality of the revolutionary taking of power, Lenin identifies *democracy* and *State*. Referring to the Marxist conception of the State 'withering away' in a classless society, Lenin writes in *The State and Revolution*:

. . . it never enters the head of any of the opportunists, who shamelessly distort Marxism, that Engels is consequently speaking of *democracy* 'dying down of itself', or 'withering away'. This seems very strange at first sight. But it is 'incomprehensible' only to those who have not thought about democracy *also* being a state and, consequently, also disappearing when the state disappears. Revolution alone can 'abolish' the bourgeois state. The state in general, i.e. the most complete democracy, can only 'wither away' (*Collected Works*, vol. 25, p. 397).

In the same work, in another paragraph in which one detects a certain contradiction with the one just quoted, he again identifies democracy and State:

. . . it is constantly forgotten that the abolition of the state means also the abolition of democracy: that the withering away of the state means the withering away of democracy. . . . Democracy is a *state* which recognises the subordination of the minority to the majority, i.e., an organisation for the systematic use of *force* by one class against another, by one section of the population against another (ibid., pp. 455–6).

I take the liberty of considering that the conception of democracy which Lenin expresses here, the identification democracy=State, and also the idea that the subordination of the minority to the majority, i.e. an organisation for the systematic use of force by one class or section of the population against another, is a restrictive conception of democracy which arose in the heat of arguments against the defenders of the 'democracy' of the bourgeois state.

Engels, in *The Origin of the Family, Private Property and the State*, refers unequivocally to the *democracy* of the period of primitive communism, of the ancient gens, i.e. he refers to *a democracy existing when the state did not as yet exist*:

And this gentile constitution is wonderful in all its childlike simplicity! Everything runs smoothly without soldiers, gendarmes or police; without nobles, kings, governors, prefects or judges; without prisons; without trials. All quarrels and disputes are settled by the whole body of those concerned – the gens or the tribe or the individual gentes among themselves. . . . All are free and equal – including the women (Marx/Engels, *Selected Works*, London, 1968, p. 519).

Engels stresses the part played among the Iroquois by the *assembly*, at which they spoke and in that way influenced decisions. Among the 'Homeric Greeks' and the Germans of ancient times reference is made to the people's general assembly, which everyone was able to address, and agreement was reached by a show of hands or acclamation. In that period, says Engels, 'spontaneous democracy was flourishing to the full'. He also refers to the 'spirit of freedom' and to the 'democratic instinct' which rendered the barbarians superior to the Roman empire.

It is true that the content of democracy has changed in the course of the various historical formations and that in some of them it disappeared or was reserved for the ruling class. But this in itself shows that it is a mistake to tie democracy to the existence of the State.

In the argumentation provided by Lenin on this subject in *The Proletarian Revolution and the Renegade Kautsky*, there are aspects which also lend themselves to confusion, since it is stated that '. . . in communist society, democracy will *wither away* in the process of changing, and becoming a habit, but will never be "pure" democracy' (*Collected Works*, vol. 28, p. 242).

Perhaps democracy will never succeed in becoming 'pure' – it would be necessary to examine closely what 'pure' democracy is – but if it is 'modified' and becomes a 'habit', it seems contradictory to deduce that because of this it *withers away*. What is transformed into a *habit*, remains and becomes *habitual*. The State also withers away but, contrariwise, it is clear in the Marxist and Leninist theses that it does not become a habit, but really does disappear.

The confusion is repeated in *The State and Revolution* when Lenin affirms that only under communism will *complete democracy* be possible:

. . . a democracy without any exceptions whatever. And only then will democracy begin to *wither away*, owing to the simple fact that, freed from capitalist slavery, from the untold horrors, savagery, absurdities and infamies of capitalist exploitation, people will gradually *become accustomed* to observing the elementary rules of social intercourse . . . to observing them without force, without coercion, without subordination, *without the special apparatus* for coercion called the state (*Collected Works*, vol. 25, p. 462).

That is to say that defending the revolutionary reality which was on the point of arising or which had arisen after the October Revolution, in face of the bourgeois 'democracy' constituting the height of social democratic aspirations, led Lenin to underestimate and belittle the generic concept of democracy and to identify it not only with the bourgeois State, which must be combated, but also with the State destined to wither away, and to maintain as well that complete democracy withers away when it becomes a habit, and to identify democracy with the elementary rules of social intercourse.

In trying to reduce to absurdity the arguments of the adversaries of the October Revolution, doesn't one fall, in actual fact, into another absurdity? Since there seems to be no doubt that also in the maximalist conception of the disappearance of the State and its replacement by what is called the 'administration of things', that *administration* will be carried out by human beings, and not by the things themselves, and will give rise to new forms of democracy.

I do not consider it rash to believe that some of these opinions have led disciples of Lenin – including ourselves, for a period – to underestimate the value of democracy and overlook clear examples of injuries done to it, and I am saying this even without reference to the monstrous aberrations of Stalinism.

The generations of Marxists who have lived through the grievous experience of fascism and who, in another order of things, have experienced Stalinist degeneration, appraise the concept of democracy in a different way, and not in opposition to socialism and communism, but as a road towards them and *as a main component of them.*

This conception is clearly seen in what Palmiro Togliatti wrote about the *Italian road* to socialism, not to mention earlier formulations of the Communist Party of Spain during the war in defence of the democratic Republic:

It is also necessary to declare [says Togliatti] that our democratic drive has been effective, and continues and will continue to be effective, precisely because we do not feel satisfied with mere changes of form, but are striving to shorten the road towards socialism. This struggle of ours gives a new content to those same democratic liberties, gives a reappraisal of the right to freedom, because these rights bring us nearer to the demands relating to well-being and economic progress; it puts parliamentarianism itself on quite a high plane; calls for profound democratic changes in the political system (development of local powers, of regionalism, etc.); and poses the problem of the adoption and development of new forms of democracy, in the factories and in the countryside, with the aim of ensuring that the changes and economic advances serve to satisfy the vital demands of the masses of the working people. Our actions directed towards ensuring that society advances to socialism are actions which give content and effectiveness to our struggle for democracy and to the entire democratic life of the country.

Togliatti links the idea of democracy with socialism and goes forward to explore new contributions to the enrichment of democracy – contributions which should be brought by socialism.

CHANGES IN THE APPRAISAL OF UNIVERSAL SUFFRAGE

In Marxist tradition and present-day Marxism there is an aspect of the debate about democracy which concerns the specific appraisal of universal suffrage. In his work on the State, Lenin, relying on Engels, declares that universal suffrage is: '. . . the gauge of the maturity of the working class. It cannot and never will be anything more in the present-day state' (*Collected Works*, vol. 25, p. 393).

For a long time this was the point of view of communists – and other Marxists – on the value of the franchise, a point of view which removed any possibility that the revolutionary forces might reach government through it. This is understandable if one bears in mind the fact that the communist parties were inspired from birth by the example of the Great October Socialist Revolution, in which the armed masses had destroyed a crumbling State without making use of universal suffrage. It is also understandable if we do not forget that our parties separated from social democracy and came into conflict with it, because in the countries where social democracy had succeeded in becoming a political force, precisely through the vote, it had not only failed to come out against the imperialist war but had supported its own bourgeoisie, betraying the International.

This negative conception of universal suffrage was regarded as having been confirmed by the experience of fascism in such countries as Germany and Italy, where Hitler and Mussolini had come to power through parliament with the connivance of other bourgeois parties and of the State apparatus, proceeding to destroy democratic liberties. The experience of fascism initially led the revolutionary forces to a profound distrust of democratic methods.

But what the experience of fascism really demonstrated – and the Seventh Congress of the Communist International took this into account – was not the usefulness or uselessness of the vote and of the democratic road, but the experience of a working class doomed to impotence by division and incapable of uniting and rallying round itself the sections of working people and the middle strata in order to confront the danger, using the resources of democracy and relying on them, likewise when it came to using force.

For finally – and this was the essence of the policy of the popular fronts in that period – the working class succeeded in learning the lesson of its need for unity and for alliance with the other sections of the working people, as well as the lesson of the intrinsic value of democratic liberties, for which it once again came to accept the most painful sacrifices.

A work of Engels, published in 1894–5, regained its topicality: his introduction to Karl Marx's work *The Class Struggles in France 1848–1850*. Engels explains that:

When the February Revolution broke out, all of us, as far as our conceptions of the conditions and the course of revolutionary movements were concerned, were under the spell of previous historical experience, particularly that of France (Marx/Engels, *Selected Works*, London, 1968, p. 644).

In the same way the communists – and not we communists alone – worked for a long time in the countries of Western Europe under the spell of the Russian Revolution without taking into account the objective conditions in which it had taken place.

But history – *Engels continues* – has shown us too to have been wrong, has revealed our point of view of that time to have been an illusion. It has done even more: it has not merely dispelled the erroneous notions we then held; it has also completely transformed the conditions under which the proletariat has to fight. The mode of struggle of 1848 is today obsolete in every respect, and this is a point which deserves closer examination on the present occasion (ibid., pp. 644–5).

Engels goes on to show that up to that time revolutions had confined themselves to replacing one definite class rule by another; they were the work of minorities confronting other minorities, in which the people intervened in favour of one of them or else calmly acquiesced in its rule. But the great mass of the people was not, except in special cases, such as the revolution of 1789, an active subject.

To that type of revolution there corresponded the struggle on the barricades, which Engels said was 'to a considerable extent obsolete'. 'Let us have no illusions about it: a real victory of an insurrection over the military in street fighting, a victory as between two armies, is one of the rarest exceptions,' he added (ibid., p. 65).

Engels gives his reasons for saying this – reasons which I am not going to repeat – and, incidentally, does not reject the possibility of revolutionary armed clashes, any more than that possibility can be entirely ruled out today, even when one comes out in favour of the democratic road, if the violence of the ruling class in a historical situation of crisis provokes it. It is certain that Engels, already at that time, was making a connection between changes in the conditions of wars between nations and the changes taking place in the class struggle.

A little earlier, however, Engels brings out the 'great service' rendered by the German workers in supplying 'their comrades in all countries with a new weapon, and one of the sharpest, when they showed them how to make use of universal suffrage' (ibid., p. 649).

The franchise has been, in the words of the French Marxist programme [says Engels], *transformé, de moyen de duperie qu'il a été jusqu'ici, en instrument d'émancipation* – transformed by them from a means of deception, which it was before, into an instrument of emancipation. And if universal suffrage had offered no other advantage than that it allowed us to count our numbers every three years; that by the regularly established, unexpectedly rapid rise in the number of our votes it increased in equal measure the workers' certainty of victory and the dismay of their opponents, and so became our best means of propaganda; that it accurately informed us concerning our strength and that of all hostile parties, and thereby provided us with a measure of proportion for our actions second to none, safeguarding us from untimely timidity as much as from untimely foolhardiness – if this had been the only advantage we gained from the suffrage, it would still have been much more than enough. But it did more than this by far. In election agitation it provided us with a means, second to none, of getting in touch with the mass of the people where they still stand aloof from us; of forcing all parties to defend their views and actions against our attacks before all the people; and, further, it provided our representatives in the Reichstag with a platform from which they could speak to their opponents in parliament, and to the masses without, with quite other authority and freedom than in the press or at meetings . . .

With this successful utilisation of universal suffrage, however, an entirely new method of proletarian struggle came into operation, and this method quickly developed further. It was found that the state institutions, in which the rule of the bourgeoisie is organised, offer the working class still further opportunities to fight these very state institutions. The workers took part in elections to particular Diets, to municipal councils and to trades courts; they contested with the bourgeoisie every post in the occupation of which a sufficient part of the proletariat had a say. And so it happened that the bourgeoisie and the government came to be much more afraid of the legal than of the illegal action of the workers' party, of the results of elections than of those of rebellion (ibid., p. 650).

Continuing his argument, Engels went on to express the view that this road was necessary in a slow and persevering effort to win over to revolutionary ideas the great mass of the people, without whose direct intervention the complete transformation of the social organisation was inconceivable.

We can count even today [Engels continued] on two and a quarter million voters. If it continues in this fashion, by the end of the century we shall conquer the greater part of the middle strata of society, petty bourgeois and small peasants, and grow into the decisive power in the land, before which all other powers will have to bow, whether they like it or not. To keep this growth going without interruption until it of itself gets beyond the control of the prevailing governmental system, not to fritter away this daily increasing shock force in vanguard skirmishes, but to keep it intact until the decisive day, that is our main task (ibid., p. 655).

That is to say, already in the last century, and on the basis of the sole and exceptional example of Germany in a Europe in which the working class was very far from constituting the force which it does today, in which the forces of culture did not count as a revolutionary force, in which the present historical experience did not exist and neither did the victory won by socialism and decolonisation in many countries, Engels attributed to universal suffrage virtues which would scandalise the 'leftist' dogmatists of today. In the same vein he adds:

The irony of world history turns everything upside down. We, the 'revolutionists,' the 'overthrowers' – we are thriving far better on legal methods than on illegal methods and overthrow. The parties of Order, as they call themselves, are perishing under the legal conditions created by themselves. They cry despairingly with Odilon Barrot: *la légalité nous tue*, legality is the death of us; whereas we, under this legality, get firm muscles and rosy cheeks and look like life eternal. And if *we* are not so crazy as to let ourselves be driven to street fighting in order to please them, then in the end there is nothing left for them to do but themselves break through this fatal legality (ibid., p. 656).

It is also in this work that Engels draws a vivid comparison between the Marxist revolutionaries and the early Christians.

Obviously, Europe and the world have changed so much since Engels was writing in this way and since Lenin looked on universal suffrage exclusively as a *gauge* of the political maturity of the working class, that we cannot keep within the same confines when we are talking about the developed countries of Europe.

Universal suffrage is not a panacea; it is not the *only* method of political action for the working people and the forces of culture; but for the reasons I have been explaining, in the Europe of today the socialist forces can enter government and come to power through universal suffrage and they will maintain themselves in a leading position in society if they are able to keep the confidence of the people through periodical elections.

SOCIALIST CRITICISM AND FORMS OF DEMOCRATIC STRUGGLE

Achieving our aims entails the development of an energetic political, social, cultural and theoretical struggle against the dominant bourgeois ideology; that is to say, developing all the action we have been talking about, so as to *turn* the State ideological apparatuses against the ruling classes and, to an increasing extent, winning the understanding and support, at least in part, of the State coercive apparatuses, which have enabled those classes, so far, to ensure their domination. This is equivalent to striving for the democratisation of economic, social, political and cultural life, for the democratisation of the State organisation and apparatus.

In this undertaking, we have to win back for the forces which are fighting for socialism the intellectual and moral values which the system of State monopoly capitalism is hypocritically trying to identify with itself and which the bourgeoisie was able to personify in another epoch, when it was a revolutionary class, but which it no longer personifies today.

It is a necessity and an obligation to *open up a breach*, to achieve a *real differentiation* between those who sincerely cherish the values of democracy and political liberalism and those for whom democracy and liberalism mean only the preservation of the property of State monopoly capital and its economic privileges. The latter are *democrats* and *liberals* so long as democracy and liberty do not call into question the economic system that is in force; when this ceases to be the case, they become fascists and are capable of murder and torture and of persecuting their own children in cold blood.

Sometimes the boundary between the two categories is not clear and they appear to be mixed. The foundation of the policy of the Centre or Centre Left which has bolstered up the European political system during this period has been based on that confusion.

What today distinguishes a genuine democrat or liberal from a diehard defender of the system of monopoly capitalism is his acceptance or his refusal of the right of the socialist forces to govern and to apply their programme if the majority of the population, through the ballot box, gives them the mandate to do so, as well as the recognition of the right of communists to function without restrictions in the democratic field.

Similarly, what distinguishes the European communist parties which have assimilated the experience of this period and which treasure democracy as it should be treasured, is their attitude towards criticism made in good faith from various quarters, their democratic style in political argument and ideological struggle, as well as their own critical attitude towards defects in the established socialist systems, and particularly towards those of their forms which are in a certain sense totalitarian – without ever confusing them on that account with the fascist regimes – and towards the underestimation of democracy, of individual human rights, bureaucratism, etc. This critical attitude is radically different from that of people who are enemies of those countries, not on account of defects in their political system, but because in them capitalist private property has been abolished and new opportunities for advance have been opened up for the exploited classes. However, our critical attitude may coincide in many respects with that of sincere democrats and liberals.

This attitude of differentiation on our part means, obviously, that we do not consider that *all* human beings are categorised politically and socially by their economic position, and this is not in contradiction with historical materialism or with the general truth that classes are defined by their social position, by their relation to the means of production. In this period of transition, just as many Christians join the progressive movement, taking their stand on Christianity's revolutionary origins, so a whole series of people, agnostics or not, undergo a similar process of evolution, basing themselves on ideas which originated in the days when the bourgeoisie was a revolutionary class with the watchword: 'Liberty, equality and fraternity.' If we fail to understand this phenomenon, we run the risk of automatically assigning to the camp of the enemies of socialism people who do not objectively belong there.

Criticism of communists' real or supposed mistakes, criticism of the negative aspects of the established socialist regimes, is not in itself counter-revolutionary or anti-Soviet. I am talking about serious criticism, not about slander. Certainly, criticism of socialist countries, if it is to be objective, must make a distinction between the objective circumstances of the different countries. In making that criticism it is necessary to take into account the history, the traditions, the development, the culture of each country. You cannot apply the same standard to Czechoslovakia or the Soviet Union of today as you would to Indochina, Korea or Cuba. But in the long run serious criticism can only strengthen socialism and contribute towards its development.

It is clearly necessary that in the established socialist regimes themselves, and above all in those which have achieved a certain level of economic development, this criticism should have internal channels through which it can be expressed, and should not be repressed by methods which turn out to be intolerable.

Socialism, in order to extend and transform itself into a world economic system – which does not imply one single model or subordination to one state or group of states, or the loss of the independence and originality of each country, or even the disappearance of differences of interests between this or that state – must recover for itself the democratic and liberal values, the defence of human rights, together with respect for dissenting minorities.

At the same time, and in the same order of things, looking upon universal suffrage as the rule, the criterion by which the government of society should be ruled, does not mean reducing the role of the masses of the people simply to voting for their representatives at intervals of x number of years. The masses must have the right to deprive their elected representatives of their mandates when they do not fulfil them, and to elect new ones. They must have the possibility of intervening at all levels of power, in the economic, social and cultural fields; this underlines the value of forms of democratic self-management and people's control.

Moreover, the mass of the people and the political forces should fully retain other rights to intervene in political life, over and above the classical freedoms of the press, of assembly, of association, etc. For instance, demonstrations and political strikes are a democratic right which cannot be given up in a truly democratic society. The only thing which should be banished from a society which is profoundly democratic is terrorism and physical violence as an instrument of political action, and the use of libel and slander against individuals or groups.

In certain circumstances, even with the existence of democratic institutions, if an elected government acts in such a way as to harm the interests of the majority in the country and to favour the privileges of a minority, the political strike is·a democratic right as a means of protest and pressure against unjust measures.

History, changes in structures, and the growth of the progressive social strata, have led to a situation in which, in a certain number of developed capitalist countries, the formula of the political general strike of the proletariat is no longer as adequate as it may once have been. In the case of political strikes, they should now bring in broader social strata, what we Spaniards have called – not from the territorial, but from the social point of view – *national strikes*. The preparation of a strike should be focused, not towards a physical confrontation with the state apparatus, but towards a democratic solution, by anticipating recourse to the ballot box, which in certain circumstances may turn out to be necessary in order to resolve serious political and social crises. This demands the ability to establish on democratic ground the aims of a strike of this kind, and from this it follows that these aims should have a broad social content, i.e. one that unifies the interests and ideas of the broadest sections.

The political strike is something very different from the strikes for particular demands which are common in the relations between capital and labour and which are generally of a limited character, being confined to one branch of industry or to a particular enterprise. The political strike is a last resort to which the people should be able to turn when, in the course of its mandate, a government moves dangerously far from the feelings and interests of society. For this reason it is indeed an exceptional step, which progressive parties should use only and always with a great sense of responsibility.

THE ROLE OF THE PARTY AND OF THE NEW POLITICAL FORMATION

The new ideas about the road to socialism in the developed countries allow certain diversifications with regard to the role and function of the Communist Party. It continues to be the vanguard party, inasmuch as it truly embodies a creative Marxist attitude. But it no longer regards itself as the *only* representative of the working class, of the working people and the forces of culture. It recognises, in theory and in practice, that other parties which are socialist in tendency can also be representative of particular sections of the working population, although their theoretical and philosophical positions and their internal structure may not be ours. It regards as normal and stimulating the competition between different policies and solutions to specific problems, and it has no hesitation in accepting, when circumstances warrant, that others may be more accurate than it in analysing a particular situation. The Marxist method is not our own exclusive property; as Marxism forms part of the universal cultural inheritance, there are parties which, from time to time and even without being aware of what they are doing, may apply it. If they are to keep their vanguard role, the communist parties must strictly carry out *a concrete analysis of concrete reality*, which at times means not only refraining from going with the stream, but swimming against it. The role of vanguard is not now a privilege derived from a name or a programme; in fact it never has been. Nor is it some sort of providential mission with which we have been entrusted by the grace of our teachers or through some authorisation from on high. It is a position which has to be earned every day, every hour, and sometimes, I repeat, by going against the stream. Either we turn our role as vanguard into a reality in that way, or else that role is reduced to an ideological fantasy which may serve to console us from time to time for our ineffectiveness.

The new ideas also mean that the party is not an army, although it is able to become one if historical conditions, the violence of the ruling classes, leave it no alternative. The party, in a democracy, is a political force made up of men and women who day by day become increasingly conscious, with a greater sense of responsibility, who freely express themselves, discuss and argue, but who agree in regarding the party's programme as their common aim; and who regard the party itself as the most valuable instrument that the working people have for their liberation, organisation as a main component of the effectiveness of political action, and unity in action and discipline – once the majority has taken a decision at congresses or in leading bodies between one congress and another – as indispensable weapons.

The men and women in the party reason and create; they are never passive elements. But they know that when the time comes for action, collective criteria take precedence over individual ones.

The party recognises that, outside collective political tasks, each member is master of his fate as regards everything affecting his preferences, intellectual or artistic inclinations, and his personal relations. It also recognises that in the sphere of theory, culture and art and in the field of research in the sciences of every kind, including the humanities, different schools may coexist within it and they should all have the possibility of untrammelled confrontation in its cultural bodies and publications. The party as such does not pass judgement except on questions of revolutionary strategy and political tactics.

The party is at one and the same time a party of masses and of cadres, of members and of militants.

The party does not set itself the aim of becoming the dominant force in the State and society or of imposing its ideology on them on an official footing. The party's mission is to contribute towards ensuring that the forces of labour and culture win political and social hegemony. With this aim, the party does not aspire to win power as a monopoly for itself, but aspires to a power in which the different political groups representing these forces take part and cooperate, according to their real weight, in emulation for progress, socialism and democracy.

It is clear that this implies a rectification of certain classical conceptions regarding the role of the party – rectifications relating to the structural changes which have taken place in society with the development of the productive forces, with the new potential correlations of forces in favour of socialism; in short, with the new realities.

In this order of things, the role which we communists used to attribute to the party in other periods as the instrument of the hegemony of the working people in society would correspond today, in the theoretical sense, to what we have called the *new political formation*.

The idea of the *new political formation* is linked with that of the hegemony of the bloc of the forces of labour and culture in society. It is certain that every social force needs a political instrument in order to play its part. We ourselves, although we have a preference for our own party, consider that it is not the only political instrument; nor are other parties, taken in isolation. The conjunction of all of them can certainly be so. That conjunction will have common characteristics and also characteristics which differ. The common features could be: a minimum programme, socialist and democratic; common bodies which would work out and study the solutions to all kinds of problems of present-day society; common bodies for political coordination and for endorsing those solutions; common action at various levels, including that of State power, in order to achieve the common aims.

The differing features might be: a philosophy or theory of its own for each party or social organisation making up the new formation; independence of its organisation, its own political life and its leading bodies; complete freedom to work out its own positions and to uphold them inside and outside the new formation; freedom to leave the new formation in the event of insuperable disagreements.

That is to say, this new political formation would be something like a confederation of political parties and various social organisations, which would act on a consensus basis, respecting the individuality and independence of each of the parties and organisations.

It would not be a super-party, since each would preserve, in the final analysis, their own freedom of action; nor would it be a merely electoral or transient coalition; it would be inspired by a desire to continue in existence in order to realise common ideals.

This new political formation is not something that can be brought about by an act of will on our part, but through a whole process of growing awareness of a common democratic road to socialism; of abandonment of positions of collaboration with monopoly capitalism, of a reciprocal coming together and the creation of a climate of confidence in which emulation will take the place of rivalry, and through forms of cooperation and common struggle at an ever higher level. In other words, it is not something which can be achieved at a stroke, immediately.

EUROCOMMUNISM AND SOCIAL DEMOCRACY

I believe that everything said so far will serve to confirm something that is important for friends and honest adversaries: that the 'Eurocommunist' phenomenon is not a 'tactical manœuvre on the part of Moscow', as some Spanish – and non-Spanish – reactionaries say. It is an autonomous strategic conception, in the process of formation, born of the experience of those concerned and of concrete reality. Anyone who judges us impartially will be bound to recognise that this strategy has not been worked out with a view to 'extending Soviet influence', nor in order to upset the correlation of military forces on our continent. In that sphere it aims at transcending the policy of blocs, at ensuring the independence of every one of our countries, and of Europe as a whole, looking towards socialism. It aims at achieving a situation in which Europe as such has a bigger say in preserving peace, international cooperation and the establishment of equitable and democratic international relations, especially with the Third World. Perhaps for that very reason, what is now commonly known as 'Eurocommunism' may be the object of anathema on one side, while on the other it is identified in a tendentious way with the opposing bloc; that is to say, it is opposed both by those who think that communism must be an instrument of Soviet policy and by those who see Europe as a simple extension of the American empire.

Although the communist tendency which I am trying to define may be valid, as regards essentials, for any developed capitalist country – as is proved by Japan – if the prefix 'Euro' can be accepted it is because, basing ourselves on the reality of each one of the countries of our continent and taking that as the starting point, the socialist forces of each state cannot detach themselves from a certain common strategy on the European level. This tendency, in order to maintain itself and achieve victory, needs coordinated action on a European scale. It is precisely this that can contribute decisively to the creation of a united Europe, standing on its own feet, bringing the continent's resources into play and making it possible for it to fulfil a role of its own within the global balance of forces, which is going through a phase of regionalisation.

On the other hand, *there cannot be any confusion* between

'*Eurocommunism*' and social democracy in the ideological sphere, not at least with social democracy as it has manifested itself up to now. What is commonly called 'Eurocommunism' proposes to *transform* capitalist society, not to *administer* it; to work out a socialist alternative to the system of state monopoly capitalism, not to integrate in it and become one of its governmental variants. That is to say, it proposes to develop the world revolutionary process, which today is an objective social necessity, in order to escape from the blind alley into which mankind has been led by the model of capitalist development.

At the same time, the 'Eurocommunist' strategy aims to bring about a convergence with the socialist and social democratic parties, with the progressive Christian forces, with all the democratic groups that are not henchmen of monopoly-type property. These aims are not contradictory, if social development is seen as a fluid and changing process and not as something static.

The historical reasons for the division between communists and socialists exist, and it is outside the scope of my intentions to make a thorough analysis of them. We communists assume full responsibility, insofar as we ourselves are concerned, for our history, with its correct judgements, its errors and its shortcomings, without disowning it or converting it into a self-congratulatory legend, but regarding it in a critical spirit.

If the socialist and social democratic parties continue, for their part, an analagous process, more or less open – for at times political parties of various kinds carry out self-criticism more by correcting their strategy and tactics than by historical analysis, at least in the first period – there is no reason for not healing the split of 1920* and arriving at a convergence on the basis of scientific socialism and democracy. A process of that kind seems to me to be the basis of the evolution which has led in France to the Union of the Left.

As for the Christian movement, there can be seen, at least as far as Spain is concerned, the development of a process of self-criticism or of an *aggiornamento* (updating) which can help to make that convergence easier.

In conclusion, the need for a dialogue between the

* The year which saw the birth of the Spanish Communist Party (*Translators' note*).

communist and the socialist or social-democratic parties of Europe, in each country and on a European scale, like that which already exists in some countries, and similar to the dialogue between Marxists and Christians started years ago, is becoming increasingly pressing, although its culmination in specific results may sometimes prove difficult and be a long process.

THE CONTEXT OF OUR DEVELOPMENT

Like the rest of Western Europe in our world of power-blocs, Spain is situated in a well-defined political, economic and military zone. We do not intend to ignore this reality. What is our position in this connection?

Our position is not to break with reality so as to go over to the other zone, to the one which, in one form or another, is grouped round the USSR. We have already indicated that our aim is a Europe independent of the USSR and the United States, a Europe of the peoples, oriented towards socialism, in which our country will preserve its own individuality.

As regards the political system established in Western Europe, based on representative political institutions – parliament, political and philosophical pluralism, the theory of the separation of powers, decentralisation, human rights, etc. – that system is in essentials valid and it will be still more effective with a socialist, and not a capitalist, economic foundation. In each case it is a question of making that system still more democratic, of bringing power still closer to the people.

The economic environment is more complicated. It is to be expected that imperialism will try to destabilise a democratic power whose leadership is in the hands of the forces of labour and culture. In face of this pressure it would be necessary to rely, in the first place, on the solidarity of the European left, in the broadest sense, not only on pressure by public opinion but also on the government policy of those countries where the left is in power; this solidarity would have to be reciprocal, integrated in a varied and many-sided process, but cohesive as regards the transformation of the social and economic structures. Hence the need for a common strategy, not only of the communists, but of the European left.

In the second place, it would have to rely on the cooperation of the Third World, especially those countries which pursue an anti-imperialist and national policy and are committed to a democratisation of international relations which will assist their development.

Thirdly, it would be necessary to strengthen economic relations with the socialist countries of Europe and Asia.

All this does not signify a transformation of our country's system of economic relations. A country's traditional system of economic relations is not changed just like that, without serious damage being done. Spain should strive to keep her historical markets, both those where she sells and those where she buys, although trying to broaden and diversify them as far as possible in accordance with her interests.

Certainly it will be necessary to support the development of our economic independence; but we realise that this independence will always be relative. We cannot shut ourselves up in the impossible autarky which was tried out and which failed under Francoism. We are in the midst of a process of internationalisation of the productive forces and are confronted with the reality of investments by foreign capital and the multinationals. A democratic and socialist Spain will have to take account of these realities and will have to try to use them in order to facilitate the country's development in those sectors which suit the national interests.

This will mean that investments of foreign capital and the functioning of the multinationals in our country will not be hindered, and consequently that foreign capital in Spain would extract profits. From the standpoint of the principles and the historical experience of socialism, this would be no more than a repetition of what has been and is being done in countries where socialism has been established for many years – countries where for a certain time economic relations with capitalist countries were actually suspended.

In the Soviet Union at one time Lenin was even in favour of granting temporary territorial concessions to foreign enterprises in order to stabilise Soviet power and develop backward areas, though it is true that this was an extreme emergency measure. In China British imperialism continues to occupy Hongkong, not because the People's Republic lacks the strength to drive it out, but because Hongkong is actually a relief valve for the Chinese economy.

At the present time, in the USSR, many banks from capitalist countries are establishing themselves, contracts are being offered to Japanese firms to organise the joint exploitation and use of Siberian gas, a subsidiary of Fiat is being established and similar agreements are being reached with companies in France and other countries. Much the same is being done in other socialist countries. And if the crisis continues to worsen in the capitalist West, its firms will compete ever more fiercely in order to conclude agreements with the socialist countries. In this way the capitalists obtain profits, but at the same time they assist in the economic development of socialist countries, for which those profits are the payment.

Comecon is trying to reach mutually-beneficial agreements with the Common Market. Socialist countries, such as Romania and Yugoslavia, are trying to become associated with the Common Market in one form or another. Poland is receiving American aid, even though that aid is small.

If things are as they are, it is obvious that a socialist democracy in Spain would have to maintain a policy of remaining open to foreign investments and to the multinationals *which suit our economic development*. In this case what would have to be preserved would be the national interest, the integration of foreign investment into the national plan, and the prohibition of any interference, direct or indirect, in internal affairs, against which the most severe economic sanctions would be justified.

In any case, it is necessary to take as the starting point the objective reality that although imperialism is no longer the only world system, there is still a *world market*, governed by the *objective laws of the exchange of merchandise* – laws that are, when all is said and done, *capitalist*.

There was a time when the political and economic leaders of the capitalist countries used to talk about two world markets: a capitalist one and a socialist one. Today there is very little talk of that kind, if there is any at all. The laws of the market, with certain exceptions dictated by the needs of political solidarity, also govern the commercial relations among socialist countries, and these countries often give preference to commercial transactions with capitalist countries because of technological advantages and favourable credits. That is to say, the socialist countries have close relations with the capitalist market – and will have closer ones as far as they are able to do so – to such an extent that although for years it was denied that the law of value prevailed in them and they theorised about this – in the formation of prices in the socialist countries, world market prices nevertheless exercise a very direct influence, although not an automatic one.

So far is this true that the crisis of the capitalist West is being directly reflected in the socialist countries. In those countries, too – perhaps with the exception of China, Korea and one or two others, whose relations with the world market are, for the time being, limited – there exists, although in a milder form than in the West, an inflationary process which is none the less real even if it is not admitted. And if in the Common Market there exists a crisis about which everyone knows, there is also evidence that Comecon is not devoid of serious contradictions either. Thus the economy, with its implacable laws, lies at the root of every political decision.

For this reason, a realistic economic policy cannot, as far as Spain is concerned, disregard the features of its economic environment. We shall have to pay a tribute in profits to foreign capital for quite a time; the important thing is to preserve our political independence while doing so and to give preference to those who do not try to use economic presence to counteract the democratic will of the people. By this we must understand not only direct pressures on a democratic government but also those which may be exerted indirectly by subsidising political parties, or the mass communications media, as often happens.

As regards the problems which arise from Spain being in an area of obvious military importance, the policy in this sphere must be flexible. It is not a question of upsetting the present world balance of forces or of switching from American to Soviet influence.

So long as an awareness of the necessity for disarmament does not impose itself, the military balance of forces may, for quite a time, be the only guarantee of peace. That is how things really are, even if it makes the present peace seem very uncertain. With this as the starting point and with the aim of non-alignment and the overcoming of the policy of blocs, one task which may be set democratic Spain is that of helping to go beyond, in the first period, the *bipolar* character of the present balance of forces and to transform it into a *multi-polar* balance. Because of this, we are not opposed to a phase in which defence is organised at a European level, independently of the United States and also of the USSR, on condition that such an organisation does not destroy the national character of the Spanish armed forces. That is to say, it is not a question of imitating Caesar's Roman legions, in which foreign forces were integrated, or Hitler's European army, in which the German general staff was in command of the forces of the countries voluntarily or forcibly associated with Germany. It is a question of an organisation which maintains the national character of each army and which has well-defined aims, the first of which should be the preservation of world peace, that of not undertaking any aggressive action against other countries and not intervening in the internal affairs of any State, whether belonging to the coalition or outside it, and not penetrating into the territory of any of them on any pretext.

In present conditions a European defensive organisation of this type could be, at one and the same time, a guarantee both for the United States and for the USSR, which moreover, because of their immense nuclear power, do not need bases or the occupation of foreign territories to ensure their defence.

5

The Historical Roots of Eurocommunism

THE POPULAR FRONTS IN EUROPE AS ANTECEDENTS OF
'EUROCOMMUNISM'

The parties included in the 'Eurocommunist' trend are agreed on the need to advance to socialism with democracy, a multi-party system, parliaments and representative institutions, sovereignty of the people regularly exercised through universal suffrage, trade unions independent of the State and of the parties, freedom for the opposition, human rights, religious freedom, freedom for cultural, scientific and artistic creation, and the development of the broadest forms of popular participation at all levels and in all branches of social activity. Side by side with this, in one form or another, the parties claim their total independence in relation to any possible inter-national leading centre and to the socialist states, without ceasing on that account to be internationalist. They devote great attention to solidarity with the countries of the Third World which are fighting against colonialism and neo-colonialism and for the increasing democratisation of international relations.

These parties are striving for cooperation and peaceful coexistence, for overcoming the policy of military blocs, for the dismantling of foreign bases, whatever country they may belong to; for the prohibition of nuclear weapons and for disarma-ment; non-interference in the affairs of other countries; and the exercise of the right to self-determination for all peoples.

These communist parties have been developing, not always at the same pace, an ideological and political fabric which distinguished them from others. Is that difference something which has happened overnight, or is it the result of a longer process with roots in the past?

The answer to this question is of some interest because, depending on what it is, it either takes away or adds substance and credibility to our present relations; and, in fact, it is true that a change of this kind always has a long period of incubation.

Yes, it would be absurd to believe that this difference has arisen overnight – whatever the forms which its political emergence has taken – in a way which is already unmistakable. For some people the differences began to become visible after the Twentieth Congress of the Communist Party of the Soviet Union; they were abruptly sharpened in 1968 with the invasion of Czechoslovakia. For others – the Japanese, for example – the critical point came perhaps at the time when the Chinese–Soviet differences began to make themselves manifest.

Already in the fifties the British communists worked out a programme in which it was envisaged that the transition to socialism would take place in conditions of democracy. This initiative preceded the period of the opening up of new horizons associated with the Twentieth Congress of the Communist Party of the Soviet Union, at which the possibility of a peaceful and parliamentary transition to socialism was established; this circumstance favoured the emergence of ideas which already existed in the minds of men like Harry Pollitt and John Gollan.

In 1956 it was the Italians, for their part, and especially Palmiro Togliatti, who penetrated most deeply into the causes of the phenomena condemned by Khrushchev at the Twentieth Congress, and into events such as those in Hungary.

Togliatti was able to put his finger on the key: *the problem lay in the political system*. Although criticism of this system was not developed (not, at least, in public), from that time on *the Italian road* to socialism began to stand out in an increasingly pronounced way.

Among western communist leaders Palmiro Togliatti was probably the one who had lived for the longest time in the Soviet Union and consequently knew it best. He had worked for many years in the small group who really took decisions in the Communist International; he had experienced the various factional struggles and had seen how they were settled. It is

probable that on more than one occasion he had been obliged
to use all his skill in order to escape from the snares and traps of
the system. The experience of the Popular Fronts, and especially
the Popular Front in Spain, the turn of Salerno,* the building of
the new Italian Republic, the territorial conflict over Trieste – in
which he took a very determined independent and national
stand – had given him valuable experience of a different kind,
which had left him better equipped than many other leaders,
above all if one adds to this his vast cultural background and his
cool and lucid intellect. From the Eighth Congress of the Italian
Communist Party onwards, an autonomous line emerged,
which Togliatti expounded to some extent at the World
Conference of 1960 and which again manifested itself in the
famous Yalta memorandum, regarded as his political testament
– an autonomous line which continued to be affirmed later
under the leadership of Luigi Longo and which culminated in
the conception of the 'historic compromise' with Berlinguer.

Already, earlier on, the Yugoslav experience had contributed
towards driving forward the trends of autonomy and
ideological creativeness. In 1948 many communist parties,
including the Spanish party, following the tradition of
unconditional support for the Soviet Union, with the
endorsement in this case of the important group of parties
which made up the Cominform, followed like a flock of sheep
the condemnation levelled against Comrade Tito and the other
Yugoslav leaders, and went so far in that unconditional support
that when Khrushchev had the courage publicly to dismantle the
whole edifice, we felt that we had been so cruelly deceived and so
vilely manipulated that this completed the demolition of what
remained of the mythical and almost religious element in our
attitude towards the Communist Party of the Soviet Union.

In the beginning workers' self-management had probably
been an ideological discovery that was rather of a defensive
character, intended to get the entire people to share in the
responsibility of construction and in the defence of Yugoslav
socialism in face of the economic and political war waged by the
socialist countries of the Cominform; but when it revealed its

* The formation of the first government of National Unity in Italy in
Salerno in April 1944, in which the Communist Party played a leading role
(*Translators' note*).

possibilities, it emerged as a very important component part of the economic and political democracy of socialism, which it was necessary to study and incorporate, insofar as it was effective, in the experience of any socialist revolution whatsoever, and which stood out as a form of self-defence against the customary bureaucratic centralism.

In going deeper into these questions, and researchers and sociologists no doubt will – if some have not already done so – a kind of dichotomy is to be seen, dating back to before the Second World War, between, on the one hand, certain of the general ways in which communist parties posed questions – even within what might be called Stalinism, with which many of our ideas were imbued – and, on the other hand, with practice, which strove to get to grips with reality and entered into conflict – sometimes one not visible on the surface – with the way in which those questions were posed.

Our opponents have often underestimated the manifestations of that dichotomy, because it has suited their own ends to do so, and have attributed them to tactics arising from particular transient situations. But anyone who knows what a communist party really is, realises full well that no transient tactics can induce it to abandon ideas which appertain to its very nature.

For instance, it would be interesting – although I have neither the time nor the materials necessary to do this – to make a thorough study of the extent to which the line of the Popular Front, sanctified in 1935, was the independent creation of certain parties, such as the French and the Spanish, and to what extent it was a Soviet contribution bound up with the need to stand up to fascist aggression against the USSR. The official historians may reflect a tendency to gild the lily and present an idyllic picture of the Popular Front. But today we do know, for instance, that between the French Communists and the Comintern there were at that time important differences regarding it. The confrontation between Maurice Thorez (who was in favour of taking part in the Popular Front government after its victory in Paris), and the Comintern (which was against this) – even though we have no detailed knowledge of the discussions to which it gave rise and even though the question was settled through the authority of the Communist

International – was not, if viewed correctly, a difference of secondary importance. It was not just a question of having or not having ministerial portfolios. It was a basic question; it concerned the content and the scope of the Popular Front. A Popular Front without the Communists taking part in the government was one thing; with them, it was another. In different conditions, within the framework of a war, this was confirmed in Spain.

It is not unduly rash to imagine that a Popular Front with Communists in the government would have made the anti-fascist struggle in France more radical. Without being in the government, the Communists played a smaller role in the Popular Front; their suggestions carried less weight than they would have done if they had had government responsibility. Léon Blum's game of swinging back and forth between right and left, his inconsistencies, to put it as mildly as possible, in relation to the Spanish Republic, would not have been the same. The Communist presence which Thorez wanted to see in the government would have meant that a more energetic anti-fascist line would have been pursued inside France; a more active and effective understanding with the Spanish Republic; and a more resolute stand on the part of French foreign policy in face of the threat of Hitlerism. I do not know whether, at the time of the discussion on taking part or not taking part in the government, matters were seen and presented in this light. However, I do believe that this would have been the natural consequence of a victory for Thorez, whereas not taking part meant supporting from outside, as in a simple electoral coalition, a wavering government incapable of pursuing a consistent anti-fascist policy, with which a game could be played on the international chess-board, permitting all kinds of zigzags and feints, depending on chance circumstances, advancing and retreating, avoiding the resolute road of radical confrontation with the Axis forces.

It is not much use speculating after the event on what might have happened if Thorez had got his way; but it is reasonable to suppose that in that event the French Popular Front would have been something different from what it was and that its ability to pursue a more resolute anti-fascist policy would have influenced the situation in Europe and probably in Spain.

Even if, because of the centralism and discipline of the Communist International, these differences were settled without difficulty in internal debate, the fact that they occurred confirms that the Popular Front policy was not simply, as its enemies have claimed, a Soviet initiative bound up with the USSR's foreign policy of defence in face of the danger of fascist aggression, and that in this policy two creative approaches met, one of them originating from the periphery, dictated by specific national realities, and distinct from the other.

There is another example which illustrates that dichotomy to which I have referred. This is the case of Harry Pollitt. At the head of the British Communist Party, he considered that the anti-fascist war began from the day when Germany attacked Poland. That was not the dominant view in the Communist Party of the Soviet Union and the Communist International at that time. The official opinion in those circles was that it was a question of an imperialist war. Harry Pollitt was obliged to leave his post as General Secretary of the British party for a time. Later, when Hitler attacked the Soviet Union, Stalin proclaimed the anti-fascist character of the war and once even admitted that it had had such a character from the beginning. Harry Pollitt was restored to his post; by implication it was recognised that he had been right. I have brought up his case because it reflects the existence of a contradiction which appeared from time to time, although in those days it did not assume the proportions of a split, between the initiative of the European parties in the closest touch with reality in their countries and with the special problems of this part of the world, and the conception of the centre, in which the position of the Soviet State was entirely dominant.

THE SPANISH EXPERIENCE: THE CASE OF TROTSKY

The case of Spain is perhaps more symptomatic, because the internal revolutionary process which our country experienced with the fall of the monarchy had its own imperatives, which it is more difficult to explain away as decisions taken from outside.

When the Republic was proclaimed, the Communist Party, then small, and as narrow and sectarian as it was militant, went out on to the streets to call for Soviets and for the dissolution of the bourgeois State. This was the period of the tactics of *class against class*, which reminds one in many respects of the positions of today's leftists, although in Spain, with the exception of extremely small and dubious groups, none of the present leftists are as leftist as we were in those days.

In actual fact that narrow and leftist line originated in the directives and resolutions of the Communist International, which condemned any agreement whatsoever with the petty-bourgeois forces that conspired against the monarchy.

Life itself showed how mistaken those ideas were, and a group of party leaders who were working where the party had been able to keep in closer touch with the masses of the people – leaders like José Díaz, Mije, Delicado and Barneto in Seville, and Dolores Ibárruri in the Basque Country – began to ask themselves questions, and it was they who constituted the basis for the new team which initiated the party's turn towards the masses. These leaders, who played such a big role in transforming the party, were fortunate in that their position fitted in with changes in the orientation of the Communist International, and they succeeded in obtaining its support. But in the elections in 1933 they took a step which went a long way in the direction of the Popular Front. This was the agreement with the left-wing forces in Malaga which made it possible for Dr Bolívar, the Republic's first Communist MP, to be elected as a Popular Unity candidate.

Later, when the Popular Front was formed and when on the Soviet scene and in the Communist International the struggle against Trotskyism was at its height, the Communist Party accepted the inclusion of the Spanish Trotskyists in the Popular Front and even collaborated with them for a time in the government of the Generalitat in Catalonia.

The requirements of political development in Spain made themselves felt more strongly at that time than the incompatibility resulting from the factional struggle in the Soviety party and the Communist International. I do not know what negotiations took place in that connection, because I was not yet a member of the party and still less a member of its leadership. But in attempting to trace the antecedents in the process of development which has led the mass parties in the capitalist countries of Western Europe to a specific conception of socialism and of independence, these seem to me to be antecedents which have a certain significance inasmuch as they demonstrate the weight of the specific national problems characteristic of these countries, even when the Comintern was still an international 'party'.

Much has, of course, been said about Trotskyism and the Spanish War and this subject is again being discussed. There is no doubt at all that anti-Communist propaganda is playing a part in this for its own ends. But this fact should not blind us or lead us to deny to persons or groups unjustly accused of being 'agents of fascism' the right to rehabilitation, however overdue.

There was a time when we communists were deeply convinced that Trotsky and Trotskyism had become agents of fascism. One cannot deny the impact of the Moscow trials, and of the astonishing confessions made at them, not only on communists, but also on impartial observers who – like ourselves – could not conceive of the infernal machine by means of which those confessions were obtained. It is true that history and the Twentieth Congress of the Communist Party of the Soviet Union have confirmed many of the atrocities denounced by the Trotskyists at the time, but to choose where the truth lay, between what they said and what Stalin and his companions said, was, as it were, a question of faith, and we chose to believe the Soviet leaders. The Soviet Union was the first proletarian State and its continued survival, for us communists, came before everything else. At that stage everything that looked like an attack on the Soviet Union seemed to us to be' objectively a service to its enemies.

On that basis it was possible for the myth that Trotsky was linked with the Nazis and was protected by American imperialism to arise and establish itself, and we youngsters of that period swallowed the official accounts of the October Revolution and of the subsequent civil war, in which Trotsky's role was passed over in silence.

The publication in the USSR, following the Twentieth Congress, of texts by Lenin in which he dealt with Trotsky's positions in an objective way, supporting them in a number of cases, and in which he gave his opinion on Trotsky's personality, without hiding its positive aspects, seemed to herald a more objective treatment of Trotsky's role in historical texts. However, that treatment has not materialised. Official historical texts have followed one after another, without giving an inkling of the truth, and they continue to be a biased manipulation of facts, which does not accord with historical reality. This has contributed towards a situation in which the October Revolution and its problems continue to be presented in the form of a sickly sweet fairy-tale, hindering those who study the working-class and revolutionary movement from getting to know its rich and contradictory history, disarming them, instead of arming them politically and ideologically.

It is high time that Trotsky's role in the Revolution was presented in an objective way and this would fit in very well with a critique of Trotskyism as a trend; Lenin did this, even before the Revolution, in the period of 'Trotsky the Centrist' and during the Revolution, when he gave his opinion on some of the positions taken up by the former People's Commissar.

This presentation of Trotsky would have to start from the fact that he represented a political tendency within the revolutionary movement and the Russian party and cannot be treated simply as a Nazi agent. What reasons can delay recognition of this today? On the contrary, the truth would help in understanding the complexity of the class struggle and in giving the younger generation a clearer picture of that complexity.

Nevertheless, it must, however, be said that Trotsky's opinions on the Spanish Revolution of 1936–9 could not have been more profoundly mistaken. Trotsky assimilated whatever was happening in Spain to the Russian model and criticised his own supporters for not following that model faithfully enough. Meanwhile the revolution in Spain showed characteristics infinitely far removed from the October Revolution of 1917 – characteristics to which I shall refer later.

Pursuing for a moment this digression about Trotskyism, I should like to refer to another problem that keeps cropping up in some circles at the present time: the subject of Andreu Nin. Andreu Nin disappeared after the putsch in May 1937 in Barcelona. One story claimed that he had been murdered by some 'parallel police force'; another claimed that he had fled to the enemy camp. Everything that has come to be known since the Spanish War, or rather all that can be deduced from what is known, undoubtedly confirms that Andreu Nin was murdered and did not attempt to escape to the enemy camp.

I am in a position to say that the Communist Party, its leading bodies, bore no material responsibility for that event and if any Communist took part in it individually – and I do not know that any did – it was done on his own account and not by a decision of the party. At that time I had already begun to take part in the work of the political bureau and whenever this subject came up, the account given and accepted by everyone was that of flight to the enemy camp. Later, in the course of friendly conversations, I asked comrades older than myself who at that time had played a much more important part than I had and might have had knowledge of which I was ignorant, and they all told me that the only account they knew of was that of the 'flight'. And I am convinced that they were telling me the truth.

How could this account that was put out in 1937 have spread and have appeared credible? Nowadays this astonishes everyone who was not actively engaged in political life during that period. They can only associate it with the persecution of the Trotskyists and with acceptance of Stalin's policy. But although that was one of the reasons, it does not provide a complete explanation of why that account was readily believed. There was something more and something very important in this connection. In May 1937 there occurred the armed putsch in which the POUM* and some sections of the anarchists took part, against the government of the Republic, which had as its Prime Minister a socialist, Largo Caballero, and which was made up of five socialist ministers, four anarchists, four Republicans, one Catalan, one Basque and two communists. We were in the midst of the war against fascism. The putsch meant opening the front to the fascist forces, since some of the troops at the front were withdrawn in order to carry out the coup and others had to be called in to deal with it.

In the midst of war, with immense difficulties, whatever the motives were – and putting the best possible complexion on them, they were utterly crazy – the putsch was a grave act of treason against the Republic, and exemplary punishment by the courts was legally and morally justified. In that context the account of Nin's flight to the fascists carried conviction, not so much because of bitter feeling against the Trotskyists, as on

* The Workers' Party of Marxist Unification, of which Nin was one of the principal leaders (*Translators' note*).

account of the very fact of what, in the midst of war, was a crime
of high treason which gave credence to the image of a POUM
manipulated by Francoism. Nevertheless, the fact is that later on
the Republic's courts only passed prison sentences on the
political leaders and on the military men who abandoned the
front and turned their weapons against the people's government. This means that Nin's death was an abominable and un-
justifiable act, but one committed against the background of a
putsch, of an act of high treason that could not be justified in
the midst of a revolutionary anti-fascist war.

THE SPANISH EXPERIENCE: THE POPULAR FRONT

What matters to me in talking about the war in Spain and the
experience of the Popular Front in this book, is to show that this
was essentially a product of Spanish reality, precisely a case of
the method of Marxist analysis being applied to a specific
situation, even though it might happen to coincide with the
general lines of an international trend. If that international
trend had been different, the actual situation would still have
brought us to a Popular Front through the very dialectics of
Spanish events.

There were very definite motives for this: the need to put an
end to the repression against the movement of October 1934,*
to achieve an amnesty and the freeing of political prisoners, to
repeal the emergency legislation and restore Republican
legality, to do battle against fascism.

Those were the essential immediate aims of the electoral
coalition formed with the name of Popular Front in order to
defeat in the electoral field the right-wing forces which were
refusing an amnesty and continuing with the repression. The
social demands recorded in the programme of the Popular
Front were very unimpressive and limited, and today might
appear to be modest even to the parties of the democratic right.

It was these causes (amnesty, an end to repression, the fascist
menace) which in the last resort, and not without hesitations,
induced Largo Caballero and the socialist left – who after
collaborating in the Republican-socialist government from
1931 to 1933, strongly disliked the idea of any pact with the

* In Spain in 1934 there was a real fascist threat, to which the workers
replied with strikes and an armed rising in Asturias (*Translators' note*).

bourgeois Republicans – to accept the Popular Front, in which the latter were naturally taking part. There is no doubt that this opposition of Largo Caballero and the socialist left to collaboration with the Republicans had a decisive influence on bringing about the situation in which the working-class parties did not take part in the Popular Front government until such time as the situation, once the war had begun and Madrid was in imminent danger, unavoidably imposed this as a necessity.

Today we may well ask whether it was not a mistake for the working-class parties to abstain from taking part, and whether their presence from the outset in the Popular Front government would not have made that government act more energetically, averting the military uprising; or, once it had taken place, if by immediately arming the people, it would have been possible to achieve throughout the whole of Spain what was done in Madrid, Valencia, Barcelona, the Basque Country and other places, nipping the uprising in the bud. We may ask whether in that way the three years of civil war and nearly forty years of dictatorship might have been avoided.

The fate of Spain and of Europe would perhaps have been different if the working class had taken a direct part in the Popular Front governments, both in France and in Spain. This consideration obviously cannot change things now and is only worth referring to in a historical context.

But to return to the subject and avoid getting lost in digressions: in face of a whole series of writers and historians who today see the war in Spain and matters arising from it almost as a simple expression of Soviet foreign policy, underestimating everything specifically Spanish, everything original in that experience and, on the contrary, trying to find revolutionary originality in a few anarchistic experiments which not only failed to introduce anything new but in fact introduced some of the most bureaucratic and dictatorial features of that period – in face of all this, I would like to emphasise what, in my opinion, was most characteristic of those years.

Beyond the myths created by Franco propaganda about *reds* and *nationalists*, about *crusades* and *communism*, myths still current in some sections of society in Spain, the truth is that in the Republican zone, in spite of all the internal problems, the divisions and even the clashes which took place – not surprising at a time of war in which so many different interests were involved and so many external pressures were brought to bear – what was experienced, with more or less numerous imperfections, was an experiment in pluralism and democracy which had nothing in common with the traditional stereotypes or with the forms which other revolutions subsequently adopted.

There was a legal government, a parliament, national autonomous institutions in Catalonia and the Basque Country (Galicia had been occupied from the very first day and remained so), parties, trade unions, youth organisations of various kinds, a free press (very free indeed in view of the war situation), and freedom of expression and assembly and freedom to demonstrate. In other words, there were forms of direct democracy, with greater or less vitality, at all levels. And over and above certain vacuous arguments about the preeminence of the war or of the revolution in the tasks of the moment – and I continue to believe that what was preeminent and indispensable, in order to carry out a real revolution as well, was to win the war, something which was mercilessly confirmed by the defeat, for the defeat was the victory of counter-revolution – what is certain is that the system of pluralism and democracy maintained itself in conditions generally most adverse to a system of that type, conditions of civil war and revolution.

Anyone who looks through the press of that period without blinkers and reads the polemics which took place between the different political and trade union groups may give his sympathy to one or the other or may even condemn them all; but he will certainly have to recognise the immense amount of freedom and the effective pluralism which then existed. It was possible to criticise, and people did criticise, the government, the parties and the trade unions. There were open confrontations between different ideas about how the war should be waged.

If anything can cause astonishment it is the extent of that freedom in such a critical situation. It is true that freedom did not exist for the supporters of those who were on the other side of the trenches; but I do not believe that anyone can criticise that when we were in the middle of a civil war.

It is true that men who held very high official posts had little to do with the work of running the war. But if Azaña was more of a thinker, a literary figure than a man of action or a Clemenceau, whose fault was that? Nevertheless, figures like General Rojo, whose antecedents were rather on the side of the right wing, socialists like Negrín, a moderate man, despite everything that has been written about him, played a most outstanding part, and many similar examples could be given.

Some people have tried to explain the preservation of democratic forms as having been due to a *requirement* laid down by the Soviet Union, whose foreign policy might have found it more convenient that the situation in Spain did not become too radical. However, this is only a partial view. Economically and socially it was difficult for radicalisation to go very far. In some respects it was taken to childish extremes – I am referring to the socialisation of small businesses and of tiny agricultural undertakings carried out by a few organisations on their own account and with coercive methods. We communists opposed these excesses as being anti-social and uneconomic and as being contrary to the broad mobilisation of the people to win the war, since the essential thing, while keeping the decisive economic levers in the hands of the authorities so as to be able to wage war more effectively, was not to disorganise the economy, and to keep broad sections of small property owners in town and countryside (whose interests coincided with those of the people as a whole) united and inspired by the Republican cause. However, I am not trying to write a historical critique or to combat this or that organisation. This is not my intention in this book.

At that time we communists were already upholding the parliamentary democratic Republic, the representative bodies of the nationalities, which brought down on us a lot of criticism from leftists. Already at that time we thought that by maintaining these forms of representative democracy, by doing the same with the bodies of the nationalities, with local government bodies, and by developing forms of direct democracy in the factories and other enterprises, by giving the working people a direct say in the running of affairs at all levels, the foundations could be laid for a democracy of a new type which would proceed to socialism.

There is a letter signed by Stalin, Molotov and Voroshilov, which says the following:

To Comrade Caballero:

Our plenipotentiary representative, Comrade Rosenberg, has transmitted to us your fraternal greetings. He has also told us that you feel resolutely inspired by the certainty of victory. Permit us to send you our fraternal thanks for the sentiments expressed and to tell you that we share your confidence in the victory of the Spanish people.

We have considered, and we continue to consider, that it is our duty; to the extent that we can, to come to the aid of the Spanish government, which heads the struggle of all the working people, of the whole of Spanish democracy, against the military-fascist clique which is in the service of the international fascist forces.

The Spanish Revolution is opening up roads which are different in many respects from the road travelled by Russia. This is determined by the difference in conditions in the social, historical and geographical spheres, the demands of the international situation, which are not the same as those which confronted the Russian Revolution. It is very possible that the parliamentary road may turn out to be a more effective procedure for revolutionary development in Spain than it was in Russia.

Taking everything into account, however, we believe that our experience, and especially the experience of our civil war, properly applied to the special conditions of the Spanish revolutionary struggle, can be of definite value for Spain. Bearing this in mind and in view of your insistent requests, which Comrade Rosenberg forwarded to us at the appropriate time, we agreed to put at your disposal a number of military specialists, to whom we gave instructions that they should give advice in the military sphere to those Spanish officers whom they would be assigned by you to help.

They were warned in a categorical manner not to lose sight of the fact that, with all the awareness of the solidarity with which the Spanish people and the peoples of the USSR are today imbued, the Soviet specialist, since he is a foreigner in Spain, cannot be really useful unless he abides strictly by his function as an adviser, and only an adviser.

We believe that you are using our military comrades in precisely that way.

We ask you to tell us, on a friendly footing, to what extent our military comrades are able to carry out the mission with which you entrusted them, since naturally only if you regard their work as positive will it be opportune for them to continue their stay in Spain.

We also ask you to let us know directly and in a strightforward way your opinion with regard to Comrade Rosenberg: whether he satisfies the Spanish government or whether it would be better to replace him by another representative.

Here are four pieces of friendly advice which we submit to your discretion:

1. It would be a good thing to devote attention to the peasants, who have great weight in an agrarian country like Spain. It would be desirable to promulgate decrees of an agrarian and fiscal nature which would satisfy the interests of the peasants. It would also be a good thing to attract the peasants to the army and to form in the rear of the fascist armies groups of guerrillas made up of peasants. The decrees in favour of the peasants might be helpful in this connection.

2. It would be good to win over to the side of the government the urban petty and middle bourgeoisie, or at all events to give them the possibility of taking up an attitude of neutrality favourable to the government, protecting them from the attempts at confiscation and as far as possible ensuring freedom for commerce. If this is not done, these sections will follow the fascists.

3. The representatives of the Republican parties must not be given the cold shoulder but, on the contrary, must be attracted, brought closer and associated with the common effort of the government. It is particularly necessary to ensure support for the government from Azaña and his group, doing everything possible to help them to overcome their vacillations. This is also necessary in order to prevent the enemies of Spain from seeing in it a communist republic and so as to prevent them in this way from intervening openly, which is the most serious danger for Republican Spain.

4. The opportunity might be found for proclaiming in the press that the government of Spain will not tolerate anyone encroaching on the property and the legitimate interests of foreigners in Spain, of citizens of countries which do not support the rebels.

> Fraternal greetings,
>
> STALIN, MOLOTOV and VOROSHILOV

21 December 1936, no. 7, 812.

Although there are some people who have seen these ideas as a tactical move by the Soviet party designed for a particular set of circumstances – and in the light of things which happened subsequently or which we came to know about later, it is possible that they are not without justification – the fact is that many of us took altogether seriously the possibility of that road, which was corroborated more or less conclusively by the Twentieth Congress of the Communist Party of the Soviet Union and which corresponds to our idea of the advance to socialism with democracy.

Few people remember that in the middle of the war the

Communist Party proposed that general elections be held so
that the citizens could elect their representatives to parliament,
and that this proposal was turned down by the other parties,
mainly with the argument that the election of a new parliament
would destroy the principle of *legitimacy* embodied, according to
them, in the parliament that had been elected before the war.
That is to say that as against the picture which some people have
wanted to give, we communists were less concerned with *formal*
liberty than with the real existence of a democratic parliament.
The same thing happened at other levels of direct democracy.
We communists always fought for the democratic election of
factory committees, coming out against the unfortunately
dominant attitudes which left the composition of those
committees to nomination from above by the trade union
bureaucracies.

During the war, and also afterwards, we communists were
criticised for our *moderation*; because we upheld the right of the
petty-bourgeois and bourgeois parties to take part in the
government and, at the very least, in political life with full
rights; because we insisted on the rights of the small and
medium proprietors being upheld; because, where we were able
to do so, we re-established religious activities; because we came
out against the multiple police forces, set up by parties and
organisations, parallel with the official police; and because we
maintained that justice must be handed out by judges, in due
legal form. If in our ranks at some time there were deviations
from these standards, we fought against them and overcame
them without hesitation. In the same way, from the very first
day, we upheld the existence of a single national army, with a
unified command and obedient to the government, instead of
the group militias; we supported the principle of making
extensive use of the abilities of professional military men, and if
so many of them, without any Marxist background, joined our
ranks, this was because they saw in the party a respect, a spirit of
organisation, a conception of the democratic state that was not
so apparent in others.

The strength that we came to have among the people came to
us, not from the fact that the weapons with which the Republic
was defending itself were almost exclusively Soviet. Other
countries since then have defended themselves with Soviet arms,
better and more effective than the ones we had, without the

communists becoming stronger because of it. That strength came from a coherent policy, *moderate* in the eyes of some, which interpreted better than other policies the sentiments most widely shared in our zone. And because *moderation* in political orientation was accompanied by a willingness to make sacrifices and a discipline at the front that led the high command – which was certainly not communist – to employ communist-led units, known to be always ready for battle in any circumstances, for the most daring offensives and most costly and crucial defensive operations.

In the war many posts were held by members of the Communist Party. That is one of the criticisms sometimes made against us. What is forgotten is that those posts were taken in the army and through promotion during the actual fighting. In the government, at most, there were two communist ministers – socialists, anarchists and Republicans held more posts. At one time there was only a single communist minister – Vicente Uribe, with the portfolio for agriculture. At the same time we communists held far fewer of the senior administrative posts than other parties; and unless I am mistaken, in diplomacy and in the purchasing commissions abroad, we had nobody at all.

What is also ignored is the fact that the Communist Party was ready, at one moment, even to give up the ministerial portfolios it did have and to support the government from outside in order to facilitate the government's relations with the Western powers, with the aim of bringing to an end its almost exclusive dependence on Soviet supplies, and that if this decision, which had already been taken, was not carried out, this was because some of our allies thought it might have disastrous effects on the morale of the Republic's fighting men.

So the Communist Party placed the cause of the people, of the Republic, above other considerations. There may have been local and individual breaches of this rule of conduct here and there, but they were rectified whenever they were discovered.

Even when the Casado coup* took place in Madrid in 1939, following the initial resistance to an attempt to capitulate to the

* In the final stages of the Spanish Civil War a group of Spanish politicians and military leaders, led by Colonel Segismundo Casado, carried out a military coup, centred on Madrid, with the aim of bringing the war to an end through what they called 'an honourable peace', but which turned out in practice to be more like unconditional surrender (*Translators' note*).

enemy camouflaged under the cloak of an 'honourable peace', which experience, or rather the death of so many men, showed later to be impossible, the party endeavoured to reach an agreement with the Casado Junta so as to carry out, at least, an organised withdrawal in order to save the army and the tens of thousands of leading personnel who died tragically and who belonged to the most widely differing organisations.

I am bringing in all this so as to show that even if certain general theoretical positions may sometimes have been out of phase with actual practice; even if many features of the content of our first ideological attitude might seem to be in contradiction with what we are saying today, a serious analysis of our actual practice, a theoretical elaboration of that practice – still scarcely sketched out in the rough – would show convincingly that the roots of our present position were already there.

It is unfortunate that traditionally theory has not been the strong point of the Spanish working-class movement. The proof of this is that men like Besteiro and Araquistain were able, at one time, to pass themselves off as Marxist 'theoreticians', without any justification, perhaps because 'in the country of the blind the one-eyed man is king'. Still today, when our ranks already contain theoretical forces who would be able to shed light on history, the dispersal brought about by underground conditions, the exhausting burden of immediate tasks, and even the difficulty of opening up a path through the tangle of falsified, distorted and subjectively-manipulated information, results in it still being difficult to carry out in a serious way the work of drawing general theoretical conclusions from all that practice.

To sum up, even if it was more through revolutionary intuition than as a result of profound theoretical elaboration and analysis, our policy in the Popular Front period already contained in embryo the conception of an advance to socialism with democracy, with a multi-party system, parliament, and liberty for the opposition. As for the excesses that took place in one direction or another, and they did take place, excesses that would have been unthinkable in a normal democratic situation, the cause of these must be sought in the passions of a civil war unleashed by the right, which opened up the deep wounds inflicted by age-old oppression and exploitation. As a result, it is not only from a Marxist analysis of present-day reality, but also from our own complex experience, that we derive the arguments in favour of the democratic socialism we advocate for our country.

THE EUROPEAN COMMUNIST PARTIES AFTER THE
SECOND WORLD WAR

Whilst there are in our past political positions features on which our present political line is based – I am referring here to the case of Spain – anyone who examines the experience of the Western European communist parties after the Second World War will see that they have adjusted their activity to democratic practices, without overstepping them at any time. In 1945 communists were taking part as ministers in all the governments of Western Europe except in Britain and the Federal Republic of Germany, and not just because the anti-Hitler coalition existed between the USSR and the western powers, although this helped, but because during the resistance to Hitlerism in Europe, the communists were in the forefront – as on every occasion when liberty had to be fought for – and thus won an outstanding position among the forces which in each country played the leading part in opening the way to victory.

The years from 1945 to 1947 were the years of the greatest democratic expansion on our continent. In 1947 the beginning of the Cold War created a new correlation of forces; there was the union between the social democratic forces and the bourgeoisie under the aegis of the United States, against the communists. Following this, the communists left the governments and went into opposition without attempting, in any western country, to hold on by force to the positions they were losing in the governments.

It will be said that this attitude corresponded to the division of zones of influence established at Yalta by the great powers. What is certain, however, is that in Greece, at that time, civil war was raging and the communists were fighting with arms in their hands against the existing authorities, who were backed by the Americans, and it seems clear that at Yalta Greece remained on the western side. In countries like Italy and France the communists were very strong and if the party had called on them to recover the arms that had been buried in the resistance, they would have done so and would have fought. Perhaps they would have been defeated, but they would have put up a considerable fight. Nevertheless they preferred to follow the democratic rules. They continued to develop a strategy directed towards unity and democracy – one which at that time might have seemed utopian – and in the course of long experience they worked out their own road to socialism based on democracy. It seems more convenient to many persons to judge the western communists by this or that phrase, or by the acts of other brother parties than by the entire road which they have travelled . –a road which has been long enough and consistent enough to provide the best of proofs.

In the course of charting the new roads, what was hardest to . accomplish was the winning of autonomy in relation to the Soviet Union. The traditional links which united the communists with the USSR had been maintained after the war, in spite of the dissolution of the Communist International, among other things because of the immense growth of Soviet prestige throughout the world, following the outstanding and decisive part played by the USSR in defeating Nazism.

The Cold War seemed, not only to communists, but also to many people who were simply progressive, to be yet another repetition of the imperialist attempts to destroy the socialist gains with fire and sword. The theories of Foster Dulles and his like bore this out. At a time when, in addition, the United States had an overwhelming nuclear superiority, the idea would not readily have occurred to any communist of breaking the bonds of deep feeling uniting him with the country of the first socialist revolution.

Nevertheless, at least for some parties, and, of course; for the Communist Party of Spain, the dissolution of the Communist International in 1943 disturbed the type of relations which they had with the Communist Party of the Soviet Union. Following that dissolution, I do not remember any turn, any important political decision about which our party consulted the Soviet party beforehand; while on some occasions, more by chance than not, because it coincided with journeys made for other purposes (Spaniards lived in emigration in the Soviet Union), we informed the Soviet Party after the event.

The actual formation of the Cominform took us by surprise and although we did not make this public, it did not afford us any pleasure. What was the significance of that step? What role was that august body, about which we had not even been consulted, going to arrogate to itself?

A revealing fact regarding the change that had taken place in practice in the relations with the Communist Party of the Soviet Union was that one month before Yugoslavia was denounced by the Cominform, a delegation of ours was in Belgrade having discussions with Comrade Tito; it would not for one moment have occurred to us to consult Moscow about this, nor did we have the slightest idea of the conflict that was about to break out.

None the less, the changes were still not great enough to prevent us from falling into the unforgivable error of supporting the Cominform's condemnation of Yugoslavia, which had been arrived at, moreover, without informing or consulting the other parties, presenting us with a *fait accompli* which we either had to reject or accept, for whoever rejected it would also have ended up by being excommunicated. During that period excommunications were still the accepted thing, and I do not believe that any party was ready to run that risk. In any case, those who had taken the initiative in setting up the Cominform had set up, together with it, a rather special kind of internationalism in which the vast majority of the communist parties were reduced to the role of supernumeraries, an 'internationalism' that is quite reminiscent of what is now called 'socialist internationalism', which puts in a privileged position the relations among a group of socialist countries – not all of them – and which, fundamentally, whatever the formal denials that may be made, aims to maintain in existence, at all costs, a world centre.

To put it simply, in the first period the dissolution of the Communist International meant for us a division of labour: '*We look after the affairs of Spain and there we hold undisputed sway. The Soviet comrades look after world affairs, for they have the experience, the information and greater global responsibility.*' It was not until later that we realised that in order to tackle and solve the problems of Spain in a satisfactory way, we also had to concern ourselves with the affairs of the world, including the socialist world.

For us, for the Communist Party of Spain, the culminating

point in winning our independence was the occupation of
Czechoslovakia in 1968. The preparations for that operation
had been carried out with methods similar to those employed in
the famous trials in 1936, which had been exposed at the
Twentieth Congress of the Communist Party of the Soviet
Union, or similar to those used in the denunciation of
Yugoslavia in 1946. That is to say, a bald statement was made –
in this case that Czechoslovakia was on the verge of falling into
the hands of capitalism – and with that statement as the starting
point, stories were concocted that were light-years away from
the truth. This was far more than we could be expected to
swallow. Czechoslovakia was the straw which broke the camel's
back and led our parties to say: 'No.' That kind of 'internationalism' had come to an end as far as we were concerned.
It is precisely to that, to what we have called the 'old internationalism', that, so far as we are concerned, an end must
be put. True internationalism is and must be something else.

I realise that writing in this way – for everyone is already
talking in this way, within four walls – lays one open to
misunderstanding and blame, but it has to be done. Why not let
us get used to the truth? Everyone would gain by it and we
should be laying the foundations for a genuine and healthy
internationalism.

If I write in this way, moreover, it is in order to establish
firmly the fact that our party – as have others as well – has arrived
at the ideas which it is upholding and developing today through
a lengthy and complex historical process, through the
application of Marxism to changing conditions. So I am doing
so in order to draw the conclusion that those who cast doubt on
the credibility of our democratic stand have not taken the
trouble to examine the path we have travelled or have a vested
interest, arising from narrow partisan motives, in not
examining it.

THE ROLE OF VIOLENCE IN HISTORY

It is true that we communists have revised theses and formulas
which we once regarded as articles of faith. It is true that long
years of struggle against fascism have helped us see more clearly
the true value of democracy – its true and, I would add, its
permanent value. It is true that we have overcome a certain

underestimation, already left far behind us, of so-called *formal liberties*. The monstrous crimes of imperialism, its obvious degeneration in all fields, have made freedom and democracy more precious to us. At the same time we have looked, without blinkers, at the weaknesses of democracy in the socialist societies in process of being born, and we have become more severely critical of deformations and breaches of democracy which we used to attribute earlier to reasons that made them seem less intolerable and led us even arrogantly to justify them in face of the class enemy.

We shall not, however, abandon the revolutionary ideas of Marxism; the ideas of the class struggle, historical materialism and dialectical materialism; the conception of a world-wide revolutionary process which is putting an end to imperialism – a process understood not as the defeat of this or that country, but as the defeat of a social system increasingly harmful to all countries, including those enabled by history to use that instrument to obtain a higher standard of living and lord it over the rest. Such a victory over an unjust system has to be supported by all countries, with their own struggle.

I am insisting on this, because some of those who see changes in our positions ask us whether we are not going back to the traditional positions of social democracy. Within our own movement, too, there is no lack of such more or less veiled accusations.

We are not returning to social democracy! In the first place because we are not in any way discarding the idea of coming to power in a revolutionary way, if the ruling classes were to close the democratic paths and a set of circumstances were to develop in which the revolutionary road would be possible. When we look at the present situation in Spain, with its specific features, we communists, aware of its complexity, declare with a full sense of responsibility that today it is possible to pass from dictatorship to democracy without the use of force. It is one of those historical situations which are not easily repeated. And we are convinced, for the reasons given, that with democracy the road can be opened up to a new model of socialism which will maintain and increase liberties, without refusing them to an opposition prepared to wage the struggle at the ballot box and in the representative institutions.

But the question of the role of violence as the midwife of history, as a theoretical question and one that was not invented by Marxism but was taken up by it from the actual experience of wars and bourgeois revolutions, from the whole process of the class struggle – this question should be dealt with at greater length.

When we in the communist parties of western capitalist countries come out in favour of socialism in democracy, are we perhaps rejecting that experience and the theoretical statements of our teachers? Are we identifying ourselves with traditional social democracy?

Certainly we are not. Violence gave birth to the bourgeois system. Without the English Revolution of 1640, without the American Revolution, without the Great French Revolution of 1789, and the changes which the Napoleonic wars introduced into social relations, extending bourgeois law everywhere, it is impossible to conceive of the leap from feudal society to bourgeois society, which constitutes such a great historical advance. The classic example of a bourgeois revolution is undoubtedly the Great French Revolution which totally destroyed the old social system and impregnated other countries with its ideas, in one way or another, over a long period. As the historian George Rudé writes, with reference to the effects of 1789:

The eventual outcome was so to transform the Europe of the Old Régime that, at the close of the revolutionary and Napoleonic era in 1815, there was hardly a country west of Russia and Turkey and north of the Pyrenees whose society and political institutions had not been profoundly affected. From this result and the events that preceded it some historians have concluded that the French Revolution was not so much a unique and particular phenomenon as merely one 'phase' of a far wider convulsion that they have variously termed a 'western', 'Atlantic', or 'world' revolution (*Revolutionary Europe 1783– 1815*, London, 1964, pp. 179–80).

Rudé himself is not in favour of these terms being applied to the French Revolution. But that revolution did undoubtedly spark off a period of bourgeois revolutions in the countries that were more ripe for them, and it was the one which achieved the most undoubted influence and the greatest repercussions.

Up to about 1848, the Great French Revolution continued to nourish the various revolutions that were carried out by the bourgeoisie with its ideas and aims. But around 1848 a new class, the proletariat, appeared in the lists, with its own revolutionary claims, and from then on, for the bourgeoisie, revolutionary violence became universally transformed into the worst of crimes. Tocqueville, for instance, found France's great bourgeois revolution logical and he formulated judgements which might give some of our present-day reformers food for thought, such as this, for instance: 'It happens most often that a people, which has supported without complaint, as if they were not felt, the most oppressive laws, violently throws them off as soon as their weight is lightened . . . Feudalism at the height of its power had not inspired Frenchmen with such hatred as it did on the eve of its disappearing. The slightest acts of arbitrary power under Louis XVI seemed less easy to endure than all the despotism of Louis XIV' (Alexis de Tocqueville, *L'Ancien Régime* (English translation), Oxford, 1937, p. 186). Yet this same Tocqueville said in a speech on 27 January 1848:

Look at what is going on within those working classes which at present, I admit, appear calm. There is no doubt that they are not stirred by political passions, properly speaking, as deeply as they used to be. But have you not noticed that their passions have been transformed from political passions into social ones? Do you not realise that, little by little, there are being propagated in their midst opinions, ideas, which do not aim at overthrowing particular laws, a particular minister, a particular government, but society itself, by smashing the foundations on which it rests today? Do you not realise that it is being said among them with growing insistence that the division of wealth which has prevailed up to now in the world is unjust, that property is based on premisses which are not just? And do you not believe that when ideas of this kind penetrate deeply among the masses, they lead, late or early, to the most fearful of revolutions?

The 'most fearful of revolutions' showed its face amid the ruins of Paris, besieged by the Prussians, in 1871: it was the Commune, the first power of the working people. But against it there united, to crush it with fire and sword, enemies who had up to the previous day been irreconcilable foes – the Prussian junkers and the French bourgeoisie.

Nevertheless, the Commune had put down deep roots. The

proletarian revolution had managed to appear in history, even if only ephemerally and precariously. The exploited classes had been taught a lesson: that the revolutionary violence of the exploited classes is a sacred right, in certain conditions, so that those classes can liberate themselves and put an end to oppressive violence; that just as the bourgeoisie, when it was a revolutionary class, had used violence in order to get rid of feudal society, so the proletariat had to have recourse to it to put an end to capitalism and move on to socialism.

Marx and Engels, the founders of scientific socialism, linked the idea of revolution with that of revolutionary violence, and in their historical conditions they were right to do so. Without the use of revolutionary violence the Great October Socialist Revolution would not have taken place and that revolution, whatever its vicissitudes, represented for the victory of world socialism as much as, or more than, the Great French Revolution signified in its day for the victory of the bourgeoisie. It was the sacrifice of the Russian working people, the October insurrection, the civil war, the role of the Soviet peoples in the war against Hitlerism that opened the way to later revolutions, to decolonisation and to the political and economic liberation of many countries; to the defeat of fascism and the preservation of democracy. Of course, other peoples fought and deserved their victory. Yet would that victory have been possible if it had not been preceded by the Great October Socialist Revolution? Would it ever have been won without revolutionary violence?

Moreover, without this as an antecedent, among other factors, *would it, perhaps, have been possible for us to set ourselves the aim today of advancing towards a new model of socialism, along a democratic road, extending and augmenting democratic freedoms?*

Émile Vandervelde – chairman of the Second International, who in that capacity criticised the Russian Revolution – wrote (unfortunately I do not have the text to hand, but I remember the gist very well) that many of the social and political gains of the working class in the West were due to the impact produced on the bourgeoisie of these countries by the victory of the Russian Revolution.

For that reason we, who do not in the present conditions accept the idea that 'the touchstone of proletarian inter-nationalism is the attitude towards the USSR' – with everything that this principle, now fallen into disuse, signifies — nevertheless cannot cease to associate with the victory of the Great October Socialist Revolution all the progressive changes that have developed in the world, and to regard it as the starting point of the revolutionary transformations which will lead mankind to socialism.

A phase of revolutionary violence was indispensable in order to break the resistance of the capitalist system, just as it was for the bourgeoisie in order to destroy the feudal system. When Kautsky was still a Marxist and when his opinions carried weight in the revolutionary working-class movement, he made fun of the social democrats 'for whom the social revolution towards which we are advancing seems to be no more than a slow transformation, scarcely perceptible, even though far-reaching, of the social conditions, a transformation such as was brought about by the steam engine' (*The Road to Power*).

THE RUSSIAN COMMUNISTS HAD NO CHOICE IN 1917 BUT TO TAKE POWER

It was certainly the case that around 1917 the view in the Marxist camp, following the analyses of Marx and Engels, was that the revolution would take place first of all in the developed capitalist countries.

Marx and Engels lived and worked at a time when the modern proletariat existed, as a class, mainly in the West European countries and America. Imperialism as a modern system had not yet taken shape, although there had been colonies and colonial exploitation for a long time. It was very difficult to imagine the victory of the socialist revolution as taking place first of all in countries other than those mentioned. There was a time when, on the basis of that premiss, it was generally accepted that 'only where the capitalist system of production has reached a high level of development do the economic conditions permit the transformation by the public power of the capitalist ownership of the means of production into social ownership' (*The Road to Power*).

But what is the specific level of production that capitalist development has to reach in order to be considered high enough? Furthermore, does the taking of power by the proletariat have to coincide mathematically with the moment when the material basis is at its optimal point? Do events happen in history in such an ideal way? Or, on the contrary, does not what some bookish Marxists have regarded as *an historical anomaly* – the taking of power in 1917 – correspond rather to the element of chance, to a particular combination of circumstances, to the imponderable element which sometimes takes over in history?

In some of their writings Marx and Engels show that they looked at this question in a much less mechanical way than some of their followers. In *The Communist Manifesto* they wrote as follows:

The Communists turn their attention chiefly to Germany, because that country is on the eve of a bourgeois revolution that is bound to be carried out under more advanced conditions of European civilisation, and with a much more developed proletariat, than that of England was in the seventeenth, and of France in the eighteenth century, and because the bourgeois revolution in Germany will be but the prelude to an immediately following proletarian revolution (Marx/Engels, *Selected Works*, London, 1968, p. 63).

I do not have precise information available about the development of capitalism in Germany in 1848, but it is obvious that it was still not so high as to make it possible to count on a proletarian revolution that did not have the support of the peasants and the petty-bourgeois strata, and indeed Marx and Engels did rely on them.

It is clear that Marx and Engels were mistaken about the possibility of a rapid transformation of the bourgeois revolutions into proletarian ones around 1848. The agreement reached between the upper strata of the bourgeoisie and the remnants of the *ancien régime* led to the defeat of the workers who, in the course of those revolutions, especially in France, raised their own socialist banner on the barricades.

Yet even in those countries most industrially advanced at that time (setting aside Britain, where no revolution took place), given the actual development of the means of production, was it not the case that a socialist revolution would have turned out to be *an historical anomaly*? In that period the proletariat did not constitute the majority of the population in any of the continental states.

Marx and Engels, who for obvious reasons were not able to study the imperialist system, as Lenin studied it later, nevertheless did not see the socialist revolution as the inexorable fulfilment of a set of rules, predetermined, in an obligatory way, for a precise level of capitalist development.

Kautsky wrote in *The Road to Power* that Engels and Bebel:

. . . taking as their basis the experience of almost an entire century from 1789 to 1871, continued to cherish the hope of an imminent revolution, which naturally would still not be its [the proletariat's] own exclusive work, but that of the petty bourgeoisie and the proletariat, which in view of its increased importance the latter would lead.

Years later, after having subjected earlier statements which regarded the revolution as being nearer at hand than it really was to a certain amount of criticism, Engels continued to think that the revolution could survive without adjusting itself to an 'historical timetable'. In this connection, Kautsky wrote that:

In 1891 Engels still thought that a major war would be a misfortune for us, because *it would involve a revolution* and would carry us to power prematurely. He believed that the proletariat, by utilising the existing political institutions, could still make more positive progress than by running the risks of a revolution provoked by war.

Kautsky does not mention the actual sources on which he bases that opinion attributed to Engels, and at the moment I am unable to make a search for them. But although in 1891 Engels may really have thought that it was better to wait for a time more ripe for revolution in the material sense, he considered, according to what Kautsky says, that war *would involve a revolution* and that the proletariat would have to take power, *even if that were premature.*

It is strange that Kautsky, probably the one theoretician most committed to the idea that *a high level of the development* of capitalist production was essential in order to go over to socialism, wrote about this opinion of Engels at a time (1909) when according to him 'the situation has changed':

The proletariat has made sufficient progress to face a war more calmly. And it would not be a case of a premature revolution, since the proletariat has drawn from the present political institutions all the strength which they could give it . . .

Yet later, in 1918, when the Russian proletariat had taken power in the conditions of imperialist war and of the collapse of the tsarist regime, Kautsky contradicted himself and contradicted Engels by criticising the Bolsheviks for acting as they had.

That is to say, when Lenin in 1917 aroused the working class for revolution and the taking of power, although the conditions of capitalist development in Russia and the ruin brought about by the war were a terrible handicap in achieving socialism – a handicap which Lenin and the Bolsheviks recognised – he was doing something the circumstances and dangers of which had already been seen by Engels, without rejecting it on that account.

We can discuss the problems of socialism attained in those conditions and the objective dangers this entails; what is beyond doubt is the fact that the Russian communists and working class had no choice but to take power and try, with the help of the European revolution, to lay the foundations of a new society.

The social democrats, who at one time relied on Kautsky in matters of theory, did not have right on their side against the Bolsheviks. They themselves had stood by their own bourgeoisie during the imperialist war, had betrayed the ideals of socialism and of the International, and were continuing along the same road by aligning themselves with the bourgeoisie against the October Revolution. So while we communists claim the Great October Socialist Revolution as the starting point leading to the new world society, in which no one will be exploited and no one will exploit, an equitable and fraternal society, the socialists of today would find it hard to claim and take to themselves the past of social democracy, if they want really to be *socialists*.

6

The Dictatorship of the Proletariat

It is appropriate to conclude by dealing with the subject of the *dictatorship of the proletariat*, a concept from which, in one way or another, a substantial number of communist parties in the West have detached themselves.

The term *dictatorship* has in itself become hateful in the course of the present century, which has seen the most abominable fascist and reactionary dictatorships, among them that of Franco, and has known the crimes of Stalinism – that is to say, the phenomena arising from the corruption of the dictatorship of the proletariat – and the evils of totalitarianism of one sort and another; all that is enough to justify the abandonment of the political use of the term. However, if we leave it at that, our opponents will be justified in accusing us of unscrupulous and superficial tactical manoeuvring or else of simply going back to social-democratic positions.

Clearly the reasons for rejecting the term are of a much more serious and far-reaching kind, and it must in general, be admitted that they have been stated but, as far as I know, never sufficiently explained, from a serious Marxist standpoint. I must confess that in attempting to tackle this subject I feel myself to be of too small a stature in face of its magnitude. I am very far from regarding myself as a theoretician. I regard myself as a modest Marxist political worker. It is precisely as a *Marxist political worker* that I cannot feel happy or satisfied in developing a political standpoint which I regard as being, *not only more advantageous, but also more correct* without trying to give it a foundation of principle, a Marxist foundation. I realise that in a territory that is relatively unexplored, as this is, I run the risk of making mistakes, not to mention the efforts that may be made to spread confusion and misrepresent my line of thought so as to discredit, not so much myself personally, but any attitude which *does not preserve* dogmas which some people look upon as sacred, thereby justifying their own immobility, for in our camp, too, there are 'immobilists'.

As regards the errors which may be discovered by those who are working, with a serious approach and with greater knowledge than mine, to develop Marxism and to bring the struggle for socialism up to date, I am open to all the criticisms which they may make of me along these lines and I admit here and now, in all humility, that there will be justification for many of those criticisms. In undertaking this work I am only putting my own judgement and my own personal responsibility at risk, although this is being done with the desire to place the strategy of the Spanish Communist Party on a firm foundation.

Palmiro Togliatti, who, among communist leaders, was undoubtedly the one who began to tackle these problems most profoundly, emphasised in his day that the task of working out the democratic road to socialism, with its own historical originality, demanded, together with practical political activity, serious efforts in the sphere of theoretical research.

I want to begin by stating categorically that although Marx and Engels publicly used the expression *dictatorship of the proletariat* only on a limited number of occasions, it is not possible to share the reformist opinion of those who attribute this almost to editorial hazard, to a chance formula of no very great importance, as might be gathered from Kautsky's pamphlet *The Dictatorship of the Proletariat*, in which there is ironic talk about '*the little words "dictatorship of the proletariat" which Marx used once in 1875 in a letter*'.

Kautsky himself, in his book *The Road to Power*, some years earlier, had written precisely the opposite and had said with reference to Marx and Engels:

. . . It is no less certain that they have created the expression *dictatorship of the proletariat, for which Engels was still fighting in 1891, shortly before his death*, an expression of the exclusive hegemony of the proletariat as the only form under which the latter exercises power.

To claim, as some people have done – and Kautsky among

them in the end – that Lenin was taking advantage of one 'little word' in order to build up an entire conception, is to reject the thinking of Marx and Engels.

MARX AND ENGELS ON THE STATE

Louis Althusser, referring to the Marxist theory of the State, calls it 'descriptive', giving us to understand by this term that it is a question of the *beginning of theory*, a beginning which 'gives us what is essential' in that theory, but which requires *further development*. In my opinion this is so, and it is so in the process of the thinking of Marx and Engels as well. They continued to go forward with the definition of their theory, in a series of successive steps, although in the very first ones there is already much of what is essential. But it is so also because of the modifications which the size and growing complexity of the functions assumed by today's capitalist State continue to introduce into its structures.

Without claiming to enter upon an exhaustive and learned examination of Marx's work, it can be pointed out that from his first writings devoted to the critique of Hegel, who presented the State as 'the reality of the moral idea' and idealised the Prussian monarchy, Marx upholds, on the one hand, political democracy, but on the other he is already tackling essential features of the relationship between the State and civil society, of the role of the State in general.

In the *Contribution to the Critique of Hegel's Philosophy of Law* (1843), Marx writes:

In monarchy the whole, the people, is subsumed under one of its particular modes of being, the political constitutions. In democracy the *constitution itself* appears as only *one* determination, that is, the self-determination of the people. In monarchy we have the people of the constitution; in democracy the constitution of the people. Democracy is the solved riddle of all constitutions (Marx/Engels, *Collected Works*, vol. 3, London, 1975, p. 29).

At a time when, in Spain, certain politicians, proceeding as if under a monarchy of the *ancien régime*, i.e. of the pre-bourgeois regime, seem to think that a constitution *vouchsafed* is going to satisfy the people's aspirations for democracy, this distinction already made by Marx nearly a century and a half ago, between that form and the form of democracy, is not without interest.

It is also interesting, in connection with arguments which will follow later, to bear in mind that in this same work Marx brings out the idea that in a *genuine democracy* the constitution ceases to be *purely political*, an idea which has to be interpreted, in my opinion, in the light of his subsequent opinion on the withering away of the State in a classless society and the assimilation which is made in *The Communist Manifesto* between the raising of the proletariat to the position of ruling class and the winning of the battle of democracy. We can also relate to this the idea expressed by Engels according to which the proletarian revolution *'would install, before all else, a democratic State and within it, directly or indirectly, the political regime of the proletariat'*.

The fact that Marx and Engels, at other times, may have subjected 'bourgeois democracy' to severe criticism and that in speaking of democracy they put the stress on that criticism and avoided the identification which, at least until the *Manifesto* – even without going deeply into an explanation – they made between the power of the working people and democracy, is due, among other things, in my opinion, to the circumstance that from the revolutions of 1848 onwards the bourgeoisie was endeavouring to deprive the concept of *democracy* of everything it possessed as a creation of the revolutionary masses of the people and was beginning to use it against the aspirations of the proletariat and even as a cover for its deals with the remnants of the *ancien régime*. That is to say, the bourgeoisie did this when historically the proletariat was beginning to establish itself as an independent class, to break free from its bourgeois tutelage; and when the formation of the proletarian party made it necessary to stress the distinction between classes, especially with respect to property, the content of State power, and the intransigent, radical struggle against bourgeois ideology and the 'democratic' manœuvring by the bourgeoisie to defend and justify exploitation.

In any case, in the *Critique of Hegel's Philosophy of the State*, Marx was already revealing the real content of the State with great clarity:

Property, etc., in short, the entire content of law and the State is the same in North America as in Prussia. The *Republic* there is thus a mere *form*, as is the monarchy here (ibid., p. 31).

In *The Jewish Question*, insisting on the essence of the State, he writes:

The limits of political emancipation are evident at once from the fact that the *State* can free itself from a restriction without man being really free from this restriction, that the State can be a *free state* without man being a free man (ibid., p. 152).

And in 1844, Marx and Engels, in *The Holy Family*, declared that the modern democratic State:

is based on emancipated slavery, on bourgeois society, the society of industry, of universal competition, of private interests which freely pursue their own ends, of anarchy, of natural and spiritual individualism alienated from itself.

But it is certainly in *The Communist Manifesto* (1848) that, for the first time and most decisively, there is expressed the fundamental idea that the State, any State, is the instrument for the domination of one class over another; that in order to transform society the proletariat must win State power, and that the State disappears, withers away, as a result of the emancipation of the working people, and with this the idea of the disappearance of classes:

We have seen above that the first step in the revolution by the working class, is *to raise the proletariat to the position of ruling class, to win the battle of democracy* . . . [my italics – S.C.]
Of course, in the beginning this cannot be effected except by means of despotic inroads on the rights of property, and on the conditions of bourgeois production . . .
When, in the course of development, class distinctions have disappeared, and all production has been concentrated in the hands of a vast association of the whole nation, the public power will lose its political character. Political power, properly so called, is merely the organised power of one class for oppressing another (Marx/Engels, *Selected Works*, London, 1968, pp. 52–3).

The Communist Manifesto already summed up the essence of Marxist theory on the State which, in its broad outlines, continues to be valid today for communists and for all socialists who want really to transform present-day capitalist society by democratic means.

The State, in democratic countries as well, is in the last

analysis an instrument of the hegemony of a class, of the dominant role of a class, in society. Even in countries where there are most liberties, the State is the organised power of one class for oppressing another.

The experience of fascism – and we Spaniards have borne the brunt of it for a long time – shows the most extreme, the most intolerable and the most repulsive aspect of a State. Under fascism arbitrary rule knows no limits; crime, torture, the physical annihilation of opponents, the denial of any active role to the classes and social groups which are not, strictly, the ruling ones, corruption and robbery, contempt for, and degradation of, culture, the absence of any ethical and moral rules – these are the laws operating in everyday life. Fascism is the most hateful form of the class domination of monopoly capital, sometimes acting in alliance with the semi-feudal remnants that survive in society.

In the struggle against fascism we communists, and others too, have confirmed that democratic liberties, even with all the limitations and restrictions imposed in bourgeois society, have a real value which must not be underestimated.

Perhaps it is the case that, having lived through that grim experience, we have achieved a better understanding of the fact that *democracy is not an historical creation of the bourgeoisie*, as we came to believe in the days when our obsession was above all else to draw a line between ourselves and 'bourgeois democracy' and affirm the class stand and class ideology of the working people in face of it.

It must be said that experience of the struggle against fascism has also led us to react in an increasingly critical way to the degeneration of that Soviet system known as 'Stalinism', and all its consequences, and to have great reservations when contemplating what we might describe as 'socialist totalitarianism'.

In reality, democracy, in various forms, antedates the existence of the bourgeoisie as such and will survive beyond class society, the State, socialism. . . . Even under communism, democracy, understood as meaning the active participation of *all* in the administration of society, will continue to be an indispensable treasure, or rather will achieve its fullest and most complete realisation.

Bourgeois revolutions – and their most classic example, the

French Revolution – had to incorporate democratic demands in their programmes, because without the support of the people, of the toiling classes, of the most lowly sections of society, they would not have had the strength required to destroy feudal domination. The people would not have fought to raise the bourgeoisie to power without the inducement of liberties. Nor does this conflict with the fact that the bourgeoisie itself needed some of those liberties for its own social development and in order to maintain its rule in a certain period.

We cannot ignore the fact that democratic liberties were a great contribution made by the most progressive forces of the people to those revolutions. Moreover, it is not by chance that throughout contemporary history it has always been the people, with the working people at their head, who have fought for liberties and most often given their lives for them.

Nor is it a matter of chance, a case of negligence on the part of Marx and Engels if in the *Manifesto,* and in other works, they come to identify *the raising of the proletariat to the position of ruling class* with *winning the battle of democracy.*

While I intend to return to this question later, what I want to emphasise here is that actually, even in the most democratic bourgeois societies, the State 'is . . . the organised power of one class'. Let us take any of the states of Western Europe – not to mention the USA! What do we see? When the working class and the progressive sections are upholding their rights, are demanding new social, economic or political gains – what do they come up against? Against a whole framework of codes and laws worked out in order to preserve at all costs the privileges of the ruling class, the system of capitalist ownership – codes and laws that make it possible to imprison and condemn those who are trying to bring about changes. In the last analysis, they come up against the forces of order, which are always provided with the most sophisticated equipment and are very highly trained in order to crush any attempt at protest.

The power of the State, moreover, has powerful means, direct and indirect, with which to condition and diminish vital liberties. For instance, when a government redivides the constituencies in a high-handed way in order to alter the actual result of universal suffrage, it may seem that it does violence only to the paper on which the administrative map of the country is printed, but in fact it is brutally restricting the right of broad sections of the population to obtain democratic representation on the representative bodies. When radio and television penetrate right into the domestic hearth with information and propaganda slanted from on high, this is not apparently an act of violence; but in reality they are inflicting a kind of lobotomy on the brains of millions of people, amputating their possibility of thinking and making up their own minds freely.

The very sharing out of State credits – and who would think of violence in this connection? – is a way of dispossessing some people in favour of others: sometimes spreading ruin and disaster among some sections in order to put small groups of monopoly capital in a privileged position. In practice, the struggle against these decisions – as we are seeing not only in a series of working-class conflicts, but also in others which affect the peasants and the small producers – is not always free from acts of bloody violence.

In the most democratic of capitalist States everything is arranged with a view to upholding the interests of the ruling class. To crown it all, in the present period, the multinationals and the imperialist powers surreptitiously and secretly intervene in other countries against the democratic and liberation movements and against governments which are simply trying to uphold national sovereignty. They maintain vast secret services in whose armoury are to be found the most varied weapons of crime and corruption. Although it may be doubtful whether what is being revealed about the CIA is a reflection of the real activity of that organisation, except to a minimal degree, the part that has been exposed is nevertheless sufficient to enable one to realise the level of violence to which *the modern State apparatuses* are capable of sinking.

Not to speak of the wars of aggression waged by US imperialism in Vietnam and against the other peoples of Indochina! In that case we find ourselves confronted with the example of a capitalist State which arrogates to itself the right to employ violence not only against the oppressed classes in its own country but also in order to enslave and exploit entire peoples, just as all the colonial empires did until very recently.

Evidently the conception of Marx and Engels about the State in general continues to be entirely correct.

Moreover, there can be no thought of transforming society without achieving State power, without the working people rising to the position of the leading force in society, to the detriment of monopoly capital, and in the service of all who live by their own labour.

The question is to decide whether this is possible without breaking the rules of democracy, while changing the content of traditional democratic institutions, complementing them with new forms which expand and establish political democracy still more firmly. We Spanish communists and other parties in the developed capitalist countries declare that *this is possible*. The argument that *there is still not a single example* of the hegemony of the working people under these forms is without any scientific value. It corresponds to the dogmatic, conservative conception that *things will always be the same* – an idea to which history has so often given the lie. Things do not have to be always the same and in the end they are certainly not always the same, even though in particular historical conditions they may have been so.

WHY THE CONCEPT OF DICTATORSHIP OF THE PROLETARIAT?

What then are we going to do with the idea of the *dictatorship of the proletariat*? Why does this conception arise – one which Marx, in a letter to Weydemeyer (5 March 1852), emphasised as one of his essential *discoveries*? The question that presents itself, in essence, is whether the working people in the developed capitalist countries can impose their hegemony without resorting to the dictatorship of the proletariat, i.e. to a more or less lengthy period of transition during which the political rights of the defeated classes and their supporters are suppressed.

It seems to me obvious that in the days of Marx and Engels, even in the most developed countries, the conscious section of the proletariat which, in a revolutionary crisis, would have been able to take power into its hands (and, in most of the countries, the proletariat as such) was a minority of the population that could only take power by force of arms and hold on to it and begin the transformation of society by *force*, i.e. by *dictatorship*.

The Russian communists found themselves in the same situation in 1917 when their proletariat, which was very concentrated and was the most conscious and most revolutionary in the world, constituted a tiny minority in the country, 'a drop in the ocean of the petty bourgeoisie', predominantly peasant.

In such circumstances the notion of the *dictatorship of the proletariat* was not just a synonym for *hegemony of the proletariat*, for *social domination* of the proletariat; the notion of *dictatorship* was the inevitable means with which to succeed in consolidating the *hegemony*, the *social domination* of the proletariat. Marx, Engels and Lenin were conscious of that reality.

In the developed countries of Europe and the capitalist world, however, the working people are today the great majority of society; and the forces of culture, with their great ideological significance and their large numbers, are drawing closer to the positions of the working class. It is plain that such a situation is very different from those in which Marx, Engels and Lenin considered the *dictatorship of the proletariat* to be necessary.

It was after the Paris Commune that Marx and Engels were talking about the *dictatorship of the proletariat*, on the basis of a specific experience and certainly also bearing in mind the lessons of the bourgeois revolutions, in which that class had imposed its dictatorship and had not hesitated to use terror.

Referring to the Commune, Engels writes something which in itself constitutes a definition of the dictatorship of the proletariat:

A revolution is certainly the most authoritarian thing there is; it is the act whereby one part of the population imposes its will upon the other part by means of rifles, bayonets and cannon – authoritarian means, if such there be at all; and if the victorious party does not want to have fought in vain, it must maintain this rule by means of the terror which its arms inspire in the reactionaries. Would the Paris Commune have lasted a single day if it had not made use of this authority of the armed people against the bourgeois? Should we not, on the contrary, reproach it for not having used it freely enough. ('On Authority' in Marx/Engels, *Selected Works*, vol. 1, London, 1950, p. 578).

And Marx, in his article 'Political Indifferentisim', likewise referring to the Commune, says:

If the workers substitute their revolutionary dictatorship for the dictatorship of the bourgeois class . . . in order to break the resistance of the bourgeoisie . . . they give the State a revolutionary and transitory form.

We communists are not disowning that historical legacy when we believe that today there are other ways and other forms for establishing the hegemony of the working people in society and for achieving political power.

Today, when we read the polemics between Lenin and Kautsky – *The Dictatorship of the Proletariat* and *The Proletarian Revolution and the Renegade Kautsky* – our approval goes without hesitation to Lenin's positions.

It cannot be denied that in Kautsky's work there are certain abstract, general arguments which, if considered apart from the context in which this work was written, might seem reasonable; they relate to the value of democracy for the proletariat and to the importance of capitalist development for the creation of a socialist economy. But bearing in mind the specific circumstances of that period – the work was published in Vienna in *1918*, in the middle of intervention by the Entente powers and when civil war was raging in Russia, in the midst of the crisis brought about in the whole of Europe by the First World War, the collapse of various monarchies, insurrections and revolts which shook the continent – Kautsky's *The Dictatorship of the Proletariat* turns out to be, above all, a skilful attempt to justify the betrayal by social democracy, which had gone over to the camp of its own respective bourgeoisies during the war and was continuing to stand by their side in face of the revolutionary upsurge. And this was being done by the man who in 1909 had declared that '*in a State as industrial as Germany or England, the proletariat would already have at the present time the strength to win power, and the economic conditions would permit it, of course, to make use of that power in order to replace capitalist production by social production*' (*The Road to Power*). The same Kautsky who added to this the following: 'universal war is approaching in a threatening way; and war is revolution. . . . And it would no longer be a case of a premature revolution. . . .' With good and sufficient reason Lenin regarded him as a renegade! If Kautsky had been consistent, should he not have confronted European social democracy and called it to account, instead of doing this to the Russian communists who, for their part, were certainly carrying out the revolution and hoping for the support of the working class of developed Europe?

In the Russia of 1917 the choice between proletarian dictatorship and democracy did not present itself; the choice was between a return to autocratic military dictatorship, with a

savage bloodbath that would have made the repression of the·
Commune by the forces of Versailles look like a picnic, or the
dictatorship of the proletariat. Power was not in the hands of the
Constituent Assembly, which the military men would have
dissolved as easily or even more easily than the Bolsheviks did;
power was possessed on the one hand by the Soviets and on the
other by the tsarist generals. That was the choice and it was
necessary to choose one or the other.

Nevertheless, Kautsky shut his eyes to that reality and
presented the democracy-dictatorship contradiction as if he had
been on another planet. For him the confrontations between the
Bolsheviks and other groups seemed as if they were mere
parliamentary jousts; as if, in Russia, there was not a merciless
war, a life and death struggle, and as if those other groups were
not linked with the counter-revolutionaries and with the
Entente, taking part in local governments created by these and
in the campaign of repression against the communists which
was being carried through in those zones – all this in the midst of
the starvation and ruin into which the country had been
plunged.

'Why must democracy be an ineffective means of reaching
socialism?' Kautsky asks himself, as if democracy existed in
Russia, as if in July 1917 the 'democratic' government of
Kerensky had not been saved at the last moment by the
communists, who came out of prison – into which they had been
put by Kerensky himself – in order to take up arms and, at the
head of the workers of Petrograd, defeat General Kornilov.

Kautsky contradicts himself on a number of occasions. He
declares that 'the will to achieve socialism is the first
precondition for establishing it'. But he adds that this 'will is
created by the big industrial enterprise'. And he insists: 'This
will arises for the first time in the masses in those places where
big enterprises are already highly developed.' 'Socialism will
start from the cities, from industry, but not from agriculture.'
Not a word about the workers' party, capable of creating in the
masses the will to achieve socialism. All those phrases were very
pretty and seemingly very scientific.

Kautsky, however, was forgetting that history often puts the
cart before the horse; that imperialism, while being a single
system, had within itself such a mass of contradictions that the

revolution was able to break its weakest links. And in Russia things happened a little differently from what the books had forecast: the proletariat first took power and then built the big industrial enterprises. In China the countryside – led, it is true, by the working-class vanguard – encircled and conquered the towns. In Yugoslavia and in Cuba, notwithstanding all the differences, something similar happened, and in Vietnam as well.

Socialism triumphed first in countries predominantly agricultural, because the revolutionary vanguard was able to combine the class contradictions with all kinds of contradictions peculiar to imperialism. There will be some who regard this as an historical anomaly. It is certainly the case that if socialism had triumphed first of all in the advanced countries, its results would have been more tangible and attractive, and would have come more quickly, for all mankind. Probably we would not have experienced the inadequacies, the distortions and even the degeneration that have occurred, although it is by no means obvious that we would have avoided others – Engels himself envisaged some of those that were possible when he was thinking that victory would come first in the developed countries.

In all the countries where up to now the working people have put an end to capitalist exploitation, they have done so as a consequence of disastrous wars provoked by imperialism and have done so in countries which – with the exception of Czechoslovakia – were completely ignorant of democracy, and some of which were emerging from colonialism and even from Asiatic feudalism. Some eminent figures in the developed countries fall into a state of elegant despair in face of what seem to them to be, rather than births, abortions of history. But if history proceeds like that, and not according to plans worked out in offices and studies, what can we do about it?

As I see it, there is no doubt that the *dictatorship of the proletariat* was an unavoidable historical necessity, just as has been the case with revolutionary violence. I would add that such an instrument might still be necessary in some underdeveloped countries where revolution may occur as a result of the response to armed aggression by imperialism or to regimes of terror and violence which at some time or other may be plunged into crisis, come into collision with the majority of society and be unwilling to give way.

On the other hand, I am convinced that the dictatorship of the proletariat is not the way to succeed in establishing and consolidating the hegemony of the forces of the working people in the democratic countries of developed capitalism. In the first part of this essay I have already tried to explain why. I am convinced that in these latter countries socialism is not only the decisive broadening and development of democracy, the negation of any totalitarian conception of society, but that the way to reach it is along the democratic road, with all the consequences which this entails.

In this sphere, and at the risk of being accused of heresy, I am convinced that Lenin was no more than half right when he said:

The transition from capitalism to communism, naturally, cannot fail to provide an immense abundance and diversity of political forms, but the essence of all of them will necessarily be a single one: *the dictatorship of the proletariat* (*Collected Works*, vol. 25, p. 413).

He was no more than half right because the essence of all the various political forms of transition to socialism is, as we can judge today, *the hegemony of the working people*, while *the diversity and abundance of political forms* likewise entails the possibility of *the dictatorship of the proletariat not being necessary*.

This discussion is not a new one in the communist movement. In the years 1946 and 1947, if I remember rightly, there must have been, at certain very high levels, and without the majority of the communist parties taking part, at least exchanges of views on the possibility of the people's democracies – which were pluralist at that time – passing from capitalism to socialism without the dictatorship of the proletariat. In some circles of our movement it was said that Dimitrov had upheld that theory and that Stalin had rejected it. What is certain is that there was a period during which no one described the people's democracies as dictatorships of the proletariat, then it began to be said of them that they were 'fulfilling the functions of the dictatorship of the proletariat', and later on this concept was openly applied to them.

It should also be borne in mind that at certain moments some Soviet theoreticians spoke of Egypt as a country where socialist transformations were being carried out, and we know that there has never been anything in Egypt that could be likened to a proletarian dictatorship.

I therefore regard it as logical that the communist and socialist parties of the developed capitalist West should establish, not just their tactics, but their entire strategy on the basis of the democratic process. And when we say this and renounce, in our countries, the dictatorship of the proletariat, we are neither wolves who are donning sheep's clothing in order to cover up sinister schemes, nor are we abandoning revolutionary Marxism in order to line up with social-democratic positions. Certainly our opponents – I am referring to the all-out defenders of the capitalist system – will always accuse us of Machiavellism, in the pejorative sense of that term. It is also possible that certain persons whom we cannot regard in a social sense as adversaries, may take a long time to understand us and may criticise us *from the right or the left*. It is our job to explain ourselves with ever-increasing clarity, being more and more thorough in working out our strategy and popularising it, and regarding this task as an integral part of our democratic road.

In actual fact the lack of democratic 'credibility' of us communists among certain sections of the population in our countries is associated – rather than with our own activity and policy – with the fact that in countries where capitalist owner-ship has disappeared, the dictatorship of the proletariat has been implanted, with a one-party system, as a general rule, and has undergone serious bureaucratic distortions and even very grave processes of degeneration.

The contradictory aspect of this is that for many years, while we ourselves were pursuing a democratic policy, we took to ourselves and defended that model as if it had been our own, without any critical attitude. This, which was justified when the USSR was the only socialist country, ceased to be so after the Second World War, when the correlation of forces on the world scene had undergone a radical change.

Because of this, the struggle for socialism is demanding with increasing urgency that there should be internal criticism in the working-class and communist movement, helping to find the correct roads for overcoming the shortcomings and errors and for arriving at an explanation of historical phenomena which still remain in a shadowy half-light.

The schema of a proletarian state outlined by Lenin in *The State and Revolution* has not been realised anywhere, and least of all in the country which has been presented to us and still is being presented to us today as the ideal model. Commenting on and developing the ideas of Marx and Engels in this work, Lenin says that all previous revolutions improved the State machine, and that what is needed is to smash it, to destroy it, and that this is the main and fundamental conclusion of the Marxist theory of the State.

With the October Revolution in the USSR, one type of State was destroyed; but in its place there has arisen a State much *improved*, that is to say, much more powerful, more organised, with mighty instruments of control – a State which, while speaking in the name of society, also finds itself situated above society.

Continuing to develop the same theme, Lenin writes:

The organ of suppression . . . is here the majority of the population, and not a minority, as was always the case under slavery, serfdom and wage slavery. And since the majority of the people *itself* suppresses its oppressors, a 'special force' for suppression is *no longer necessary!* (*Collected Works*, vol. 25, p. 419).

Nevertheless the new State which arose out of the revolution did find itself obliged to create *a special repressive force*. And under Stalin that force ended up by controlling everything – society, the remainder of the State apparatus, including the army, the party, and even stretched out its arm to the people's democracies, where it carried on the repression, organising the monstrous trials at the end of the forties and the beginning of the fifties.

Lenin also used to speak about the bureaucracy and the standing army as parasites on the body of bourgeois society, engendered by the internal contradictions which tear this society apart, but in particular parasites which block up its vital pores.

Nevertheless, the State created by the October Revolution had to organise a bureaucracy and a standing army; it gave that bureaucracy privileges which exceeded the ordinary wage of a worker and made it in practice as irremovable as the functionaries of a capitalist State.

Later, Lenin himself wrote the sharpest criticism of that bureaucracy and of the dangers of bureacratisation. In other words, of that ideal proletarian State which he had imagined as one in which the armed proletariat, the people's militia, functionaries regarded as mere 'book-keepers' and paid as workers and subject to recall, were going to replace the bureaucracy, the standing army and the special repressive organisations – there is still not a glimpse to be seen, after more than fifty years in power. In its place there has grown up, above society, a powerful State apparatus which is anything but the 'cheap government' of which Lenin dreamed.

If all States are instruments for the domination of one class over another and if in the USSR there are no antagonistic classes and objectively there is no need to suppress other classes, then over whom does that State exercise domination?

The October Revolution has produced a State which is evidently not a bourgeois State, but neither is it as yet the proletariat organised as the ruling class, or a genuine workers' democracy.

Within that State there grew up and operated the Stalin phenomenon, with a series of formal characteristics similar to those of the fascist dictatorships. I stress that these were *formal* characteristics, because the essence of the Soviet regime was and is fundamentally opposed to fascism, and this is not merely a theoretical assessment but was vouched for with the blood of the peoples of the USSR during the Second World War. In addition the revolutionary essence of the Soviet regime has been reaffirmed repeatedly in solidarity with the peoples who have fought against fascism and imperialism.

For a long time, with the formula of the 'cult of the individual', we attributed those phenomena to the personal characteristics of Stalin, and it is certainly true that they played a big part in this. We Marxists do not deny the role of individuals in history. But why was it that an individual with Stalin's characteristics, even though they had been condemned by Lenin, succeeded in imposing himself? It is true that Stalin knew how to exploit, with consummate skill, the contradictions that existed between the different groups that took shape within the leadership of the Communist Party of the Soviet Union, how to set himself up as the unifier and proceed to get rid of anyone able to obstruct his rise. Yet we must ask ourselves whether the practical significance of Stalin was not more in keeping with *the type of State* which was actually taking shape, with the objective realities that surrounded him, than was the case with his opponents, especially from the moment when illness reduced Lenin's possibilities of action and then caused his premature death.

It is clear that the Stalin phenomenon, which has been a form of totalitarianism extensively exploited by capitalist propaganda, has weakened the democratic credibility of the communist parties among a section of the population in our countries.

The condemnation of the Stalinist horrors, pronounced by Khrushchev, temporarily broke up the entire system erected by Stalin, both in the USSR and in the socialist countries of the East. Events followed in Hungary and Poland, where there was formed, spontaneously and tacitly, a heterogeneous 'national front' against the Stalin system of rule. Whereas in Poland there was a communist opposition to that system, capable of rectifying the situation, this did not happen in Hungary. It was Soviet troops who restored 'order': a fresh blow against the international prestige of communism and one which also had repercussions as far as our own parties were concerned.

There were a number of years during which Khrushchev personified a new spirit of receptiveness towards the outside world and of greater freedom inside the country. This coincided with successes such as the launching of the first Sputnik, Gagarin's journey into space, new currents in Soviet literature and cinema, a cleaning up of the special repressive bodies and greater supervision over them. This was a period which resulted in a rise in the international prestige of the Soviet Union; however, it came to a speedy end.

Khrushchev was deposed by a sort of palace coup. His mistakes were 'exposed', when we had all come to believe that at last there was a collective leadership jointly responsible for good and ill. It is true that under Khrushchev's leadership there had arisen the conflicts with China – conflicts which he treated, in the light of what has since been emerging, with unquestionable levity and lack of awareness and with methods somewhat redolent of Stalin.

In actual fact, one of the causes of Khrushchev's downfall may have been his inability to transform the State apparatus created under Stalin, the *system* of political power to which Togliatti had referred and which eventually crushed Khrushshev. That system has not been transformed; it has not been made more democratic and it has even retained many of its aspects of coercion in relations with the socialist states of the East, as was brought out with brutal clarity by the occupation of Czechoslovakia.

The massive and annihilating repression of Stalin's day has ended. Khrushchev, deposed, died at home in his bed. There has been progress, tarnished by forms of oppression and repression in certain fields – and naturally in that of culture. Yet we still do not find ourselves looking at a State that can be regarded as a workers' democracy.

This affects the credibility of our party more, much more, than if the *dictatorship of the proletariat* really existed in the USSR. If *bourgeois democracies* have much that is purely *formal*, this is also true of the *workers' democracy* so far achieved by the communists.

Saying this may be regarded by some comrades, who refuse to admit the truth, as constituting a crime of lèse-internationalism. Yet nowadays, in the working-class and communist movement, these questions are being raised more or less openly, according to the given circumstances and not 'under the influence of bourgeois propaganda' as the conformists are in the habit of saying, but because the evidence of reality imposes itself. And how can we communists, who rightly regard ourselves as a vanguard force, be the last to admit this evidence, to face up to reality? Moreover, to face up to it is the only way to render service to the cause of socialism, both in the countries which have suppressed capitalist property and in those which maintain it.

That type of State which has arisen in the Soviet Union, which is not a capitalist State, since it does not uphold private property, but which is not the State which Lenin imagined either – with the workers exercising power directly – how is it to be fitted in with the Marxist conception of the State? Lenin used to speak about the State in the first phase of socialism keeping much of the content of bourgeois law. But the State with which we are dealing has gone further than Lenin foresaw in this sphere. It has kept not only some of the content of bourgeois law but has provided examples of distortion and degeneration which at other times could only be imagined in imperialist states.

At the same time, I stress that in a series of world problems this State has served the progressive policy proper to the Soviet social system. It is a question of two contradictory features which are not mutually exclusive and it is not possible to take account only of one of them on its own, if one wants to make an objective analysis.

All this raises a series of problems of political theory and practice which it is in the interests of all supporters of socialism, and in the first place the Soviet comrades, to tackle and clarify accurately and boldly. Its consequence is that the problem of the State continues to be the great problem, not only before, but also after private property has been suppressed.

WHAT TYPE OF STATE?

As regards the essential part of this question, I do not consider myself to be in a position to give a satisfactory answer. I want, however, to note down a series of facts for more general and more advanced reflection on this subject.

The great figures of Marxism spoke of two phases in building communism: the first, socialist phase, is summed up in the classical formula, *to each according to his work*; the second, the phase of communism, is expressed by the phrase, *to each according to his needs*. To the first corresponded the creation of the proletarian State, which would constitute the broadest democracy for the working people. The second phase, communism, would see the extinction of the State which, in Engels's phrase, would finish up in the museum of antiquities. together with the distaff and the bronze axe.

In practice, however, things have turned out to be much more complicated. What is serious is that we are continuing to apply to practice, which is more complex, the same theoretical schemes, as a result of which ideological reflection is moving further away from reality and is coming into contradiction with it. This moving apart of ideology and reality give to the former an alienating, mystifying character, typical of the relations between ideology and practice in bourgeois society. The manual or intellectual worker who has still not succeeded in receiving *according to his work*, who is living in difficult conditions, who is the victim of bureaucratic structures, who is kept away from all important decisions which, in one form or another, are imposed on him by the State-party duo which for him sums up authority and the power of making decisions – that worker, who has not yet emerged from alienation, cannot feel that his life is already being lived under socialism, even though private capitalists are not exploiting him. When as justification he is offered ideological schemes drawn up when only prophetic generalisation was possible, these do not satisfy him and he may begin to have doubts about socialism. It is even worse if he is told that the work of building communism has begun. Then he consoles himself with the jokes which circulate so widely in some socialist countries, and also begins to underestimate the real and undoubted progress which has been made by the society in which he is living – progress which, while it is no more than an important advance – is presented as *developed socialism* and even *communism*.

Alexander Solzhenitsyn, now roaming the world with the trappings of one of those priests of the Russian Orthodox Church, half mystical prophets, half rogues, who centuries ago used to set out on the roads of Russia to announce the end of the human race, the Apocalypse, terrifying credulous and backward peasants and making a living in that way – this man, compared with whom Peter the Great might seem a dangerous revolutionary – may be the extreme expression of disappointment and despair carried to the pitch of the most ungovernable hatred, brought about by the fact that the dream is out of phase with the reality. But the existence of such people leads one to fear that the absence or inadequacy of a Marxist critique of reality – because the State system does not provide channels that are open for this – may finish up by swelling the ranks of an anti-socialist opposition which might 'throw out the baby with the bathwater', and prevent or seriously hinder the growth of forces capable of modifying the situation along socialist lines.

It is necessary to return to the complexity of this situation and to the way in which it is in contradiction with simple schemes.

In those drawn up by Marx and Engels, apart from the two phases mentioned (socialism and communism), no account was taken of another in which the power of the State created by the revolution would have to tackle the realisation of *primary capitalist accumulation*, indispensable for undertaking modern production. That is to say that no account was taken of the fact that the new State might find itself compelled to carry out, before anything else, a *typically capitalist* task which could not be accomplished in a short period and the content of which did not undergo a fundamental change just because it was given the name 'socialist accumulation'. We know of the suffering brought about under capitalism by the primary accumulation which, as Marx explains, meant the expropriation of the direct producers, the destruction of private property based on one's own labour, the unbelievable exploitation of the labour of women and children, the heaping together of millions of families in the manufacturing countries in subhuman conditions, and the plundering of the colonial peoples.

We must ask ourselves whether the type of State which developed in the Soviet Union, and in particular the dictatorial system associated with the name of Stalin, with all its excesses, abuses and arbitrary acts, was not the consequence of that function which consisted in carrying out primary accumulation, in developing modern industry at all costs. It was certainly the case that a section of the working class and of the youth – the most conscious section – took part in that work, accepting immense sacrifices, inspired by revolutionary enthusiasm. Out of that endeavour came some of the best works of early Soviet literature and cinema – works which gave rise to waves of revolutionary romanticism all over the world and which kept the faith of millions of workers in the Russian revolution burning brightly. That sphere of determination and revolutionary energy persisted, in spite of everything, in the days of Stalin and, together with the great material and cultural achievements of that period, is the reason why it is wrong to see only the reverse side.

That reverse side consists in the fact that the accumulation, the titanic effort to develop modern industry, demanded huge and endless sacrifice from the working population – sacrifices which wide sections of that population were not in a position to accept. That was the flaw which affected the alliance between the workers and the peasants and inevitably led to the establishment of a type of State which not only repressed the former ruling classes but also a section of the people, and certainly alienated a numerous section which did not accept those sacrifices and, objectively speaking, was available to be mobilised against the new government.

The phenomena of bureaucratisation arose not only from the tradition of the tsarist State but also from this situation, which had not been foreseen by the theoreticians. Marx, Engels and Lenin himself had imagined the dictatorship of the proletariat as a power in which the vast majority repressed a tiny minority and in which the organisation of broad working-class democracy was even the very precondition for this. In practice, things did not happen in this way. A large part of the population was passive, and a very important section was hostile. Workers' democracy continued to shrink and the same process occurred within the party, in which the sharp contradictions in society were reflected in an exacerbation of factional struggles which, after Lenin's death, no one was able to control. In that way there developed a bureaucratic stratum which proceeded to absorb the functions of leadership, convinced that it was the depository of the social mission of the working class, the embodiment of the dictatorship, but which was imperceptibly putting down roots, with its own interests and acting in accordance with its own specific mechanisms and objective laws.

In a speech which he made at the First All-Russian Congress of National Economic Councils on 28 May 1918, Lenin said:

We do not shut our eyes to the fact that in a single country, even if it were a much less backward country than Russia, even if we were living in better conditions than those prevailing after four years of unprecedented, painful, severe, and ruinous war, we could not carry out the socialist revolution completely, solely by our efforts (*Collected Works*, vol. 27, p. 412).

The same idea was repeated on other occasions and Stalin, when Lenin was dead, recognised for a time that it was impossible to build *complete socialism* in a single country, and that it would only be achieved when the revolution had triumphed in other developed countries.

What relation was there between, on the one hand, this idea, which was afterwards ideologically abandoned, in order to proclaim at the Seventeenth Congress, in 1934, the victory of socialism in the USSR (which did not prevent the greater part of the delegates to that congress from being physically eliminated on Stalin's orders, or the ill-famed trials from taking place) and, on the other hand, the characteristics of the State built in the USSR.

That State no longer serves capitalist property, which has disappeared in the USSR. In that aspect, the bureaucratic stratum cannot be regarded as a capitalist *class*. It does not possess private property and the part of the profit from Soviet enterprises which goes into its upkeep is certainly less than it costs to maintain the bureaucracy in any capitalist country. Nonetheless, the bureaucratic stratum, at its various levels, wields excessive and almost uncontrolled political power. It takes decisions and settles questions over the heads of the working class, and even of the party, which, taken as a whole, finds itself subjected to that bureaucratic stratum.

At this stage of social development we are confronted with a State which sets itself above society, a State that is relatively *free* in relation to society, which does not mean that society is as yet free.

The present Soviet State has certainly carried out the functions of achieving development in the economic, industrial and cultural fields, and in the field of health, and also in that of national defence. In other words, it has carried out tasks which in other countries of advanced capitalism have been carried out by the capitalist State. Having suppressed capitalist property, it has created the conditions for going over to evolved socialism. The question that now arises is whether the actual structures of that State have not been transformed, at least in part, into an obstacle to evolved socialism; whether that State, as it now exists, is not in itself already a brake on the development of a real working-class democracy and, in addition, whether it has not constituted a brake on the country's material development.

The question is whether that State, which is no longer capitalist, is not an intermediate phase between the capitalist and the genuine socialist State, in the same way as the absolute monarchies were an intermediate phase between feudalism and modern capitalist parliamentary democracies; a phase which through analysis of its characteristics and its functions, would enable a more objective and scientific explanation to be given of the Stalin phenomenon and others like it.

The question is whether that State does not demand of the Soviet party and Soviet society a serious and profound transformation, so as to convert it into a real workers' democracy, into the kind of socialist State which the founders envisaged.

There is no doubt that in one way or another this conception has made an impression on the Soviet leaders themselves, even if only in the shape of the recognition of the inadequacies of socialist democracy. In Khrushchev's day, the thesis was developed of 'the State of the whole people', which is no longer being stressed today. But the confusion between party and State seems to lead to the creation of ideological images which cover up a reality that does not succeed in providing satisfaction, rather than to a real transformation of that reality.

I do not believe that I can fully explain, let alone solve these problems. I am only drawing attention to the need for theoretical research which can provide a basis for political options and which is in the interests of the whole of the working-class and progressive movement and, in the first place, in the interests of the Soviet comrades and those in a similar situation. That is to say, perhaps what is lacking is the political analysis of the system which Khrushchev was unable to make or did not know how to make at the Twentieth Congress and which could be the starting point for a new leap forward on the part of the Soviet Union and all the socialist countries.

THE WORLD ENVIRONMENT AND ITS INFLUENCE ON THE STATE

Another factor to be borne in mind in order to analyse the characteristics of the type of apparatus of the Soviet State is the international environment within which it developed.

The accelerated industrialisation which reduced the possibilities of democracy and led to the utmost pressure to achieve the capitalisation necessary for this goal, was not a free choice made for purely internal reasons. It was imposed to a great extent by the imperialist encirclement, by the threat of a

war which did not break out until 1941 but which had been
constantly planned against the USSR in the previous years.
Either industrialise or perish: that was the dilemma, which was
confirmed by fascist aggression.

Through that threat the imperialist powers, whether
consciously or not, exerted an influence on the whole internal
development of the USSR. They forced the pace of
accumulation and industrialisation, which necessarily limited
social measures and exerted a negative influence on agriculture;
that is to say they imposed a pace which, in the last analysis,
obstructed the alliance between the workers and peasants and
reduced the mass basis of the system. At the same time, this
situation encouraged the development of a State situated over
and above society, in which the coercive aspects assumed vast
proportions, and favoured the excesses of the Stalin period.

All this confirmed the impossibility of building *complete
socialism* in a single country without socialism also triumphing in
a series of developed countries.

In a different international situation the process of
industrialisation might perhaps have been slower, the social
transformations in agriculture less hectic – thereby preserving
allies – and the living conditions of the masses might have
improved more rapidly, thereby creating more favourable conditions for the flowering of democracy of the working people.

World conditions forced a choice on the Soviet leaders – that
of transforming the new State into a great military power and
sacrificing many things for that goal. This also gave to the State
born of the October Revolution, subsequently developed by
Stalin and continuously imprisoned in this dilemma, specific
features more likely to accentuate its authoritarian character.

Not even the breaking of the encirclement, when the number
of socialist countries was increased after the Second World War,
brought about any essential modification of the situation. The
new revolutionary States also arose in countries which were
economically backward, with agriculture predominating, and
which needed to industrialise themselves. The only one which
was at a modern capitalist level, Czechoslovakia, had achieved
this in complete dependence on the capitalist countries of the
West. On losing the markets, capital and raw materials of these
countries, Czechoslovakia did not find an effective substitute in

the East and did not prosper economically as the capitalist countries did which had been on a level with her in 1936.

The model of the Soviet State was extended almost automatically to the new socialist countries. Under the influence of Stalin's policy, 'solidarity' and 'internationalism' were applied in such a way that the independence of those countries was seriously impaired, as was recognised after the Twentieth Congress. In those countries the *variety of forms* which Lenin had foreseen for the transition to socialism was purely *formal*. In 1968 the Soviet military occupation of Czechoslovakia revealed, on the one hand, the crisis which that country was undergoing as a result of the mechanical application of the Soviet model and, on the other, the conservatism and power politics characteristic of the system.

There is no doubt that the world arms race, continuing in spite of détente, objectively tends to accentuate the coercive aspects in the Soviet State, and that the maintenance of a level of strength sufficient to withstand that of the United States demands an immense financial effort, to the detriment of social and economic progress. Even the positive aspects – if they can be called that – which the arms race may have in technological development and which in the United States are disseminated and commercialised more rapidly in other branches of the economy, facilitating their development, do not have the same speedy consequences in the Soviet Union, because of the rigidity of planning, the separation of the defence industry, and the obsessive introversion of the military sector.

Moreover, even today the imperialist States, and particularly the USA, are in a position, if not to determine, then certainly to influence a good number of Soviet decisions, not only by military pressure but, above all, with the weapons of commerce and technology.

The speeches, issued by the State Department, by Sonnenfeldt and Kissinger at a meeting in London of United States ambassadors in December 1976 are significant in this respect.

Although in many respects they impute to the relations between the Soviet Union and its allies features which more properly belong to those between the USA and its allies, and although they explicitly recognise the limits of American strength and the fact that the United States today does not have sufficient power to dominate the problems of the new correlation of forces on the world arena, there are other opinions which, even when they are wide of the mark, still have a basis of truth. For instance, the judgement that the USSR's status as a super-power is mainly based on its military strength and that a skilful and long-term American commercial policy can influence Soviet policy, given the problems of the USSR's economy and those of the other socialist countries.

The context within which the global confrontation presents itself today does not favour the transformation of the Soviet State into a State of working-class democracy. It is a context of force which puts in the forefront the role of the army and of the forces which assist it; a context in which the tendency is rather to affirm uniformity than to favour discussion; to consolidate authority rather than develop democracy. A State in which the army and the organs of authority have such an important role, even though it is a State without capitalists and even though it supports the struggle of peoples for their liberation, does run the risk of regarding strength as its first aim. It tends to convert ideology into an instrument of power; to see the problems of the class struggle, of the struggle for liberation, the struggle for socialism, on a world scale, as complementing its strength in the global confrontation in which it is involved; to see in internationalism something which reinforces its strength and to make it into an instrument.

Instead of recognising the limitations which its objective situation, the conditions in which it has developed – and its own errors and shortcomings – have imposed on its internal social transformation, on socialism's specific mission of liberating the working people and thereby freeing mankind from all oppression, from all alienation; instead of recognising how much still remains in the structures of its State that is a heritage from the old State, alien to the transitional State foreseen by the founders of Marxism; that is to say, instead of recognising that we are only trying to advance towards conditions in which socialism can expand, because history has not allowed us more than this, it is claimed that we already find ourselves in complete socialism, even approaching the first steps of communism and that no other socialism but this is possible. Moreover, to uphold this an attempt is made to maintain what we call the *old internationalism*; i.e. that which assesses communist and workers' parties by their unconditional support for the Soviet Union: 'The touchstone of proletarian internationalism is the attitude towards the Soviet Union.'

We in the communist parties which are functioning in the capitalist countries cannot accept the idea that the victory of socialism is determined in the confrontation between the countries in which capitalists no longer exist and those which still preserve capitalism. The world of today is different. Helmut Sonnenfeldt of the US State Department admitted this:

So the Soviets will be seen and heard on the world stage no matter what we do. . . . We have to get away from seeing détente as a process which appeases or propitiates Soviet power. We have to see our task as managing or domesticating this power. That is our central problem in the years ahead. . . . Our challenge is how to live in a world with another super-power, and anticipate the arrival of a third super-power, China, in 20 years or so (Speech at US Ambassadors' Meeting in London, December 1976; summary in *New York Times*, 6 April 1977).

If in the past, in some countries, the revolution was victorious as a result of military defeat, which made it easier for the working people to remove the ruling classes responsible for that defeat, this does not mean that an identical road has been mapped out for us. *We want neither wars nor military defeats between the capitalist world and the socialist world. It is not a question of the East inflicting a military defeat on the West. The question must be removed entirely from this nonsensical context. The removal of the capitalists as the ruling class must be carried out in each country, and each people must do this on its own account, with its own efforts, without losing its national identity. The role of the communists in the West is not to strengthen the military bloc of the East; it is to carry out the political and social transformation in their own countries, without this meaning that the country concerned is weakened thereby; it is to struggle to prevent war, to achieve cooperation on an international scale, based on the interests of the peoples and on democratic relations among them, and not on relations of oppression; to strive for the limitation and destruction of nuclear weapons, for disarmament and peace, for the simultaneous disappearance of blocs and foreign military bases.*

The socialist revolution in the capitalist West should involve the defeat

*and the political and social removal of the exploiting classes; but not the
national defeat of those countries by foreign powers.*

With the victory of socialism, by bringing to these countries a
further development of the historic democratic gains,
eliminating the exploitation of man by man and establishing
equitable and fraternal relations, *we communists shall work for the
strengthening, the advance of the country of our birth, so as to cooperate in
that way in the progress of mankind and not in any way to subordinate our
countries to others.*

Already today our struggle against imperialism foreshadows
our desire for democratic relations on an equal footing, and not
relations of subordination, with all countries, whatever they are,
for the future. We shall never mortgage our independence to
anyone, for the sake of any ideological or material interests.

In Kissinger's speech at the US Ambassadors' Meeting there
are a number of interesting statements which confirm the purely
capitalist content of American policy and have the merit of
throwing aside the hypocritically democratic camouflage:

There are people who think that we are too intransigent in our attitude
towards these western communist parties. But we cannot encourage
the progress of these parties nor permit the setting of a precedent in
which, by our inaction, we have facilitated the success of a communist
party. *The extent to which such a party follows Moscow's line is unimportant.
Even if Portugal had followed the Italian model, we would still have been
opposed.* It is not just because Cunhal is a Stalinist that we are in
opposition. Even the impact of an Italian Communist Party that
seemed to be governing effectively would be devastating – on France,
and on NATO too.

It is difficult to see how we could have NÁTO discussions if these
various communist parties of Western Europe did achieve control of
governments. We could, as with China, perhaps have parallel policies.
But the alliance, as it is now, could not survive. *The western alliance has
always had an importance beyond military security (New York Times,* 7 April
1977; S.C.'s italics).

Kissinger *dixit.* For him the question is not whether a
communist party 'follows Moscow's line', which, as he sees it,
means acting as a component part of Soviet power; he even
supports, for instance, the idea that the Yugoslav communists
should be 'less disagreeable' towards Moscow. In reality, the
equilibrium of military strength does not matter to him; that

equilibrium is now determined, not so much by alliances, or even by bases, as by the development of nuclear strength. Those alliances may vanish but the equilibrium will remain. What he is concerned about is that the social system should not change in Western Europe – for that reason the alliance has always gone 'beyond military security'. He does not look at the alliance in terms of military defence but in terms of the military pressure of the alliance against the social changes which each country may want to introduce in a democratic way.

The admission is important also because it torpedoes certain oversimplified dogmatic arguments according to which an independent position with regard to the USSR is equivalent to an approach to US imperialism, whereas in fact American imperialism is more worried by an independent and democratic stand by a communist party than by a follow-my-leader dogmatic one, for with this latter approach it will be hard for a communist party to reach, and above all to *continue to hold*, governing positions in a developed country in the capitalist West.

To return to the earlier argument, *the posing of the struggle for socialism in terms of a world confrontation between two systems, and in practice between two powers or two groups of powers, is not something which we favour.* Firstly, because the socialism which has been achieved up to now, still in a very preliminary stage, is not as yet the shining example that can determine victory within the framework of an ideological confrontation – I am speaking of the developed capitalist countries, to which we can propose this model – and secondly, because a military confrontation would be suicide for both sides.

That the international working-class and communist movement is not homogeneous and that different tendencies exist in it is a fact which we ought to accept. There exists – to simplify matters – a tendency having as its standard-bearers the Soviet comrades, which tries to keep the movement firmly attached to a series of dogmas which may constitute a propagandist assessment of the system arrived at in the USSR, but which, except in rare cases, does not help the communist parties to transform themselves into governing parties and, still less, into leading parties in their countries; in addition, there is also a Chinese tendency that is very difficult to define, since up to now it has manifested itself almost exclusively in an attitude of inflexible hostility towards the Soviet Union and in practice underestimates the role and independence of the international working-class movement.

And there is – to simplify, I repeat – a new tendency, which has arisen mainly in the advanced capitalist countries, which remains faithful to the principles of Marxism, which takes to itself, *in a critical way*, the gains made by the revolutionary movement so far, which strives to incorporate in the successes of theory the analysis and elaboration of structural, economic, social and cultural changes, and which demands democratic roads and independence in order to work out its own strategy.

Within this heterogeneity, of different tendencies, the national factor, as is logical, has its influence. At this stage of détente and cooperation, national forms of class struggle – and not of class collaboration – are bound to occupy a primary position, and an influence is exercised by the degree of political and theoretical maturity achieved, on a greater or lesser scale, by parties which have their own long and rich experience of class struggle.

Here are the foundations for a simultaneous cooperation and contradiction with regard to the Soviet State: a cooperation which springs from its social regime, which is not capitalist and in which the material foundations exist for the development of socialism; a contradiction which springs from its type of State which, because of its characteristics, tends to place itself above its own society and above the societies of other countries, a type of State which tends towards coercion through a series of objective and subjective factors, some of the causes of which I have attempted to outline.

The progress of the socialist movement in the developed capitalist countries may help Soviet society and the Soviet communists to go beyond that type of State and make progress in transforming it into a real working people's democracy. This is a historical necessity which would do a great deal of good to the cause of socialism throughout the world and would uproot and destroy a great deal of bourgeois propaganda. For that reason it is all the more lamentable that the Czech comrades were not allowed to carry on with their experiment in 1968.